Fish in the Bible

Psychosocial and Cultural Analysis of Contemporary Meanings, Values, and Effects of Christian Symbolism

Carmen M. Cusack
Nova Southeastern University

Vernon Series in Language and Linguistics

www.vernonpress.com

In the Americas:
Vernon Press
1000 N West Street,
Suite 1200, Wilmington,
Delaware 19801
United States

In the rest of the world:
Vernon Press
C/Sancti Espiritu 17,
Malaga, 29006
Spain

Vernon Series in Language and Linguistics

Library of Congress Control Number: 2017934980

ISBN: 978-1-62273-235-7

Cover art: Zulu

This book is dedicated to King Zulu, known as Bhoja, twin of Adee and Charaka. King Zulu wrote Fish in the Bible with me in my time of need and greatest despair. He lives on in spirit – his spirit lives!

Acknowledgments

Save the White Tiger!!!

White Tiger (Bengal)

6500 Magazine St.

New Orleans, LA 70118

1 (504) 861-2537

Table of Contents

Introduction

Fish in the Bible: Psychosocial Analysis of Contemporary Meanings, Values, and Effects of Christian Symbolism contemplates why and to what extent tales and truths about fish presented in the Bible are relevant in Christian societies. *Fish in the Bible* argues that portraits of fish and fishermen presented in the Bible have been both embraced and rejected by contemporary cultures with primarily Christian constituents (e.g. American culture). This book does not make an ethical or moral argument about whether the meaning of fish in the Bible ought to be relevant; rather, it explores manners in which Christians have selectively rejected or accepted depictions and symbols of fish and fishermen. For example, this book will demonstrate how humane slaughter methods continue to be as relevant today as they were when kosher laws were first established (Cusack, 2011). It explores differences between Christian maxims presented in Bible verses and beliefs and actions of societies operating under Christian moral majorities.

This book is holistic and nuanced. Chapters are standalone works, yet an audience member would benefit by seeing the chapters as a congruent work, not solely piecemeal supplements. By seeing the entire work, the continuity emerges and the theme is clearly established. The topic is unique, but this does not mean that it departs from traditional disciplines or authorities. *Fish in the Bible* draws from varied sources, which are essential for this type of analytical foray. Variety between chapters and diverse reference sources do not disrupt, but positively contribute to and influence, the continuity of the theme overall, which is that Christians view fish through a psychosocial lens that relates to the Christian experience as described by the Bible.

Christians may recognize their differences and experience them as being vast philosophical, social, cultural, or theological distinctions; however Christians' differences may be subtle or imperceptible to people, who differ from Christians, such as Hindus, Muslims, Buddhists, and Jews. Christianity is described as being a "body" (1 Ephesians 3:6, 5:23; Colossians 1:18-24; Corinthians 12:12-27; Romans 12:5). This metaphor is apt because an arm does not appear to be similar to a leg, but each individual is recognized as being one continuous organism. Therefore, the Christian body appears to be one organism to other bodies; and many times Christians experience it to be one body without labeling it as such. Differences between Christians are organized and fleshed-out through sectarianism, knowledge of which requires specific education, information, and experience atypical of practitioners of other religions and people living in regions that are predominantly influenced by other religions.

Fish in the Bible works on several specialized topics to argue that, overall, depictions of fish and fishermen in the Bible significantly shape Christian culture even when Christians ignore, overlook, or dismiss ways in which fish and fishermen are characterized and treated in the Bible. Fish serve as a metaphor for God's power, human sin, and fertility; they are used to instill boundaries and standards in practitioners with depictions of work and ritual; and sometimes fish are worshiped, demonized, and subjugated. There is no clear or singular message regarding fish or fishermen; and Christian societies are left to abide by a patchwork of representations to formulate their own opinions and judgments.

Fish in the Bible also considers the evolution of symbolism and metaphors in Christian society using parables and tales found in the Bible. Subsections in this book summarize and synopsize implications raised by symbolism and literalism in certain contexts, stories, and verses demonstrating potentially pervasive significances of fish in Christian cultures throughout the world. The foundations of this research are media studies, law, history, cultural studies, religious studies, animal studies, criminal justice, sociology, and environmental studies. In particular, social and behavioral patterns, as well as cultural customs, commerce, and current events demonstrate Christians' understandings of how fish and fishermen and fisherwomen ("fishermen") ought to be treated.

In considering the meaning of fish in Christian societies and culture, this book will propose that some Christians' sociopolitical and psychocultural values vary depending on innumerable factors, such as economy, geographic location, culture, and holidays. Therefore, interpretations will fluctuate based on perceptions of Christian customs, definitions of sin, and relative prices for harming or endangering species. For example, Irish American Margaret Sanger, Planned Parenthood's founder, has been blamed by Christians for corroding society's support for traditional family structures, but she explained that she and her father perceived socialism to be the purest distillation of Christian values (Sanger, 2004). "*Father never talked about religion without bringing in the ballot box* (Sanger, 2004, p. 23). *"He took up Socialism because he believed it Christian philosophy put into practice, and to me its ideals still come nearest to carrying out what Christianity was supposed to do"* (Sanger, 2004, p. 23). Sanger's father was an idealist. " *Unceasingly, he tried to inculcate in us the idea that our duty lay not in considering what might happen to us after death, but in doing something here and now to make the lives of other human beings more decent*" (Sanger, 2004, p. 23). *"[O]ne of his maxims"* was " *'You have no right to material comforts without giving back to society the benefit of your honest experience*" (Sanger, 2004, p. 23). "*[H]is parting words to each of his sons and daughters who had grown old enough to fend for themselves were, 'Leave the world better because you, my child, have dwelt in it.' This was something to live up to*" (Sanger, 2004, p. 23).

Her father's belief in socialism may have been utopian, but Sanger pragmatically attempted to put these values into practice through advocacy, debate, publication, and legal reform. Sanger believed that anti-birth control dogma could not be defended using *"nature"* because then activities, such as fishing, would also be called into question (Cusack, 2015; Sanger, 2004, p. 412; U.S. v. Stevens, 2010). "*It had become part of my routine to answer every challenge to the cause, just as I tried to answer every question at a meeting. Here again was the hoary 'nature' argument which should have been in its grave long since*" (Sanger, 2004, p. 412). Sanger argued that "*[t]he contention that it was sin to interrupt nature in her processes was simple nonsense. The Pope frustrated her by shaving or having his hair cut. Whenever we caught a fish or shot a wolf or slaughtered a lamb, whenever we pulled a weed or pruned a fruit tree, we too frustrated nature*" (Sanger, 2004, p. 412). Sanger's argument was extensive. "*Disease germs were perfectly natural little fellows which had to be frustrated before we could get well. As for the alleged 'safe period' which Rhythm now set forth, what could be more unnatural than to restrict intercourse to the very time when nature had least intended it?*" (Sanger, 2004, p. 412). Sanger's analogies and ideology continue to be unpopular among millions Christians living in capitalist societies even though pharmaceutical companies earn billions of dollars in profit from birth control policies and legal reforms pioneered by Sanger. Some corporations may even claim that their fortunes not only attest to the moral correctness of birth control and capitalism, but also to their pre-destined salvation; and in a few cases, some corporations have suggested that their prosperity correlates with faith in traditional interpretations of *"family"* that exclude birth control (Burwell v. Hobby Lobby, 2014; Weber, 2002). On the opposite extreme, numerous Christian nations are socialized, such as France, Sweden, and Canada. They provide free and low cost birth control, which may demonstrate their compassion for the masses supposedly cared for by Jesus in the Bible (e.g. feeding the multitudes by distributing five small barely loaves and two fish in Matthew 14:13-21).

Margaret Sanger and Planned Parenthood helped expand the Fifth Amendment right to privacy to include reproductive rights (Ayotte v. Planned Parenthood of Northern New England, 2006; Gonzales v. Carhart, 2007; Planned Parenthood v. Casey, 1992; Planned Parenthood v. Danforth, 1976; Roe v. Wade, 1973). Planned Parenthood, which primarily promotes contraception not abortion, has criticized liberalization of family planning rights (Bellotti v. Baird, 1976; Cusack, 2012; Eisenstadt v. Baird, 1972). Privacy rights, including, procreation, contraception, and abortion, have been developed using precedence from constitutional case law, such as Pierce v. Society of Sisters (1925), which struck down a law requiring children to attend public school after nuns sued the government because it violated parents' rights to choose how to educate and train their children. Sanger's socialistic disavowal of Catholicism was Marxist, insofar as it was revolutionary; insinuated a denial of Catholicism; and "blasphemed" the Church (Cusack, 2016; O'Hare, 2016). However, her renegade activities continue to be viewed by many Catholics as being more akin to Sinead O'Connor, who disavowed aspects of her own religion on *Saturday Night Live* when she tore a picture of Pope John Paul II and has "rallied" against the Catholic Church for more than 20 years (O'Hare, 2016).

At the beginning of the new millennium, a publication in Canada foresaw socialistic doctrinal and attitudinal shifts in the contexts of traditional Catholic rigidity, the utopian placebo, and a capitalist undertow (Ruge & Marx, 1973). *"The spirituality behind those Lenten practices was based on a dualism that set in opposition the church and 'the world,' the former ruled by Christ, the latter by the devil"* (Seljak, 2001). *"The church" was "concerned" with "the spirit, not the material world, the soul and not the body. Only by conquering the body could the soul be liberated. That is why it was so important to conquer" "appetites"* for fish (Seljak, 2001). The author could *"no longer see how"* Christians could *"sustain"* the *"'Christianity against the world' spirituality in its traditional form*, and, drew a parallel with *"the temptations of Christ"* (Seljak, 2001). In an *"optimistic culture, Christian asceticism was seen as a"* behavioral *"manifestation of a Christian neurosis: self-negation"* (Seljak, 2001). *"[M]any pressed Christianity into the service of self-esteem building"* (Seljak, 2001). The result was manufactured *"theology of hope"* (Seljak, 2001). The synthetic thrust *"was the religious equivalent of the 'I'm okay, you're okay' psychology of the time"* (Seljak, 2001). Despite nonchalance and plastic optimism, it *"was a necessary corrective to the overly spiritual and oppressive Catholicism"* (Seljak, 2001). It infiltrated heavy attitudes that for too long had made *"people guilt-ridden, neurotic and passive in the face of poverty and injustice"* (Seljak, 2001). Some Christians were *"happy to be liberated from it"* (Seljak, 2001). One negative effect is that *"culture of optimism, especially with regard to human progress, has dulled"* believers' *"sense of sin"* (Seljak, 2001). People *"create systems"* to *"serve"* personally beneficial *"interests and defend them as being in the interests of humanity. One need only listen to those who promote globalization of the free market to see"* the blatant substitution of self for the greater whole (Seljak, 2001). *"With this expanded consciousness,"* forsaking *"consumerist desires makes sense"* (Seljak, 2001). Christians *"tithe for the sake of the poor, not for the sake of" "souls"* (Seljak, 2001). Self-denial, which is the practice of *"following Jesus' example of self-sacrifice, becomes an affirmation, not a negation, of God's creation and our humanity"* (Seljak, 2001). Sacrifice *"make much more sense in the light of consumerism, racism, militarism, the widening gap between rich and poor, and, worst of all, the fact that we as a global community are moving" "from rather than towards solutions to these problems"* (Seljak, 2001). Despite immense consensus that capitalism and socialism may embody and facilitate Christianity, some Christians have implemented other political regimes, such as populism (e.g. in Venezuela) and fascism (e.g. in Germany and Spain); and have even positioned a Christian church as the official state church.

Often, the spirit of the law in diverse political systems may be interpreted according to Christians' beliefs in good and evil; and legal responses in nearly every functional political system may be based on some religious principles. Yet, the Bible was edited, influenced, and written by an untold number of contributors, who likely possessed distinct points of view that are braided into more than 31,000 verses. Like Sanger's father, who espoused the golden rule found in Matthew 7:12, some progressive Christians may promote rehabilitation and second chances; however, the golden rule is not a foundational maxim of law and policy in Christian societies. More relevant are notions of restoration and retribution based on *"eye for an eye"* described in Exodus 21:23-28, but challenged in Matthew 5:38. These distinct approaches to law and justice illustrate how moving and interlocking factors cause individuals, families, adherents, and nonreligious members of societies founded on Christian history literally and symbolically to become living interpretations of Biblical narratives and principles.

Fish in the Bible analyzes relevant cultural reflections on Biblical stories such as Jonah and the whale, Jesus feeding the multitudes, the miraculous catch, and Noah's ark, which have been imparted as children's allegories. These tales bring to life scholarly knowledge about ancient fishing industries and current fisheries and fishermen. *Fish in the Bible* thoroughly engages timely concerns such as animal rights, conservation, and poverty to look at fish as friends, foes, and food.

Chapter 1

Jonah

The tale of Jonah and the whale is well-known throughout various cultures, which have reshaped and adopted the tale. In some narratives Jonah is depicted as a hero and in others, he is depicted as a coward, who matures and comes to God because of his experiences. The whale is depicted as a fish, a servant of God, and as a beast. In some accounts, Jonah fears the fish. *"Jonah has been portrayed in Rabbinic texts as having asked the great fish to consume him"* (Goodhugh & Taylor, 1943, p. 760). In some accounts, Jonah, the fish, and God knowingly work together to achieve a mission. The Bible does not describe the fish as unknowing, unwilling, mean-spirited, hungry, mindless, hateful, accidental, unconcerned, remorseless, reticent, or any other negative quality. The Bible says that when Jonah had been hurled into the sea, he was overcome by waves, seaweed, and the prospect of death, so he prayed and God sent a fish to swallow him. *"Then they took Jonah and threw him overboard, and the raging sea grew calm"* (Jonah 1:15). God *"provided a huge fish to swallow Jonah, and Jonah was in the belly of the fish three days and three nights"* (Jonah 1:17). Jonah was sheltered by the fish for three days and nights, and then the fish vomited Jonah onto the shore when God commanded. *"From inside the fish Jonah prayed... 'In my distress I called'"* to God, who *"'answered me....I called for help, and you listened to my cry'"* (Jonah 2:1-2). *"[C]urrents swirled about me; all your waves and breakers"* (Jonah 2:3). Jonah repeatedly attributes his circumstances to the "other" (i.e. *"you"*) (Jonah 2:2). Because the sailors believed that he needed to be sacrificed to calm the sea, a reader may interpret Jonah as blaming God and attributing his perilous surroundings to God or resulting from God's commandment. *"The engulfing waters threatened me, the deep surrounded me; seaweed was wrapped around my head. To the roots of the mountains I sank down; the earth beneath barred me in forever. But you,...my God, brought my life up from the pit"* (Jonah 2:5 6). Jonah acknowledges that he may have lost sight of God before his trip, while on the boat, or after hitting the open waters. *"When my life was ebbing away, I remembered you, Lord, and my prayer rose to you....Those who cling to worthless idols turn away from God's love for them"* (Jonah 2:7-8). Jonah learns the value and meaning of his mission to Nineveh while drowning. He may have been shouting from fear or for help while drowning in a storm, but he says that he *"will sacrifice to you" "with shouts of grateful praise"* (Jonah 2:9). He *"vowed"* to *"make good"* to thank God for saving him (Jonah 2:9). Jonah was then vomited by the fish. The fish intentionally or unintentionally may have been obeying the will of the Lord.

Varying tales demonstrate how diverse interpretations may be. Ministers and scholars have extracted meanings and variations from single words, phrases, places, themes, and historical data. They have not changed the story as much as adopted a style of interpretation typical of Biblical scholars and Christians reading the Bible. Some Christians tend to interpret the Bible in a fun way—in a way that suits them (Habermas, 1987). This is an acceptable part of contemporary Christianity. Christian preachers may change stories to suit their parishioners. For example, some may describe Jonah as a prophet even though the book of Jonah may not refer to him using this word (Finger, 2015). Another example is that the original recording describes "*the leviathan as being twisted"* (Goodhugh & Taylor, 1943, p. 760). Some scholars have deduced that the original Hebrew identified a crocodile. As unlikely as this may have been *"due to crocodiles' reclusive nature and their unwillingness to interact or interfere with humans,"* the interpreter is free to assume that the fish would have been a crocodile because Christian tradition and culture allows this interpretation (Goodhugh & Taylor, 1943, p. 760). This is particularly true because original Biblical texts are not written in most Christians' native tongues (e.g. English). Due to linguistic and social interpretations, the leviathan proposed by some Christians may be much larger than a crocodile; and it may be a dragon or sea dragon described in Job 3:8 and Isaiah 27:1 (Easton, 2005). Therefore, it is possible *"that the crocodile, and not the whale, is spoken of in Genesis 1:21*" (Goodhugh & Taylor, 1943, p. 1357). "*The word in Job 7:12 must also mean crocodile. It [a]scribes some...animal, [who]...would be very destructive*" (Goodhugh & Taylor, 1943, p. 1357). "*[T]ranslators render it dragon in Isaiah 27:1, where the prophet gives this name to the king of Egypt: 'He shall slay the dragon that is in the sea.' The sea there is the river Nile, and the dragon the crocodile"* (Goodhugh & Taylor, 1943, p. 1357). Diverse interpretations may reflect distinct regional and national heritages among Christians, which may manifest in their imaginations and stories.

Christians' deductive reasoning may result from their environments, which elucidate factors that seem possible and identify characteristics in animals that would have been complementary to God's mission for Jonah. For example, to portray Jonah being a hero and coward, some Christians may suggest that a serpent fulfilled God's command (Genesis 3:12-14; Psalms 24:106). Several species of serpents live symbiotically with humans, for example, as pets or as working snakes. Commentators have suggested that the leviathan was whale, but pods may be unlikely to swim in the Mediterranean or nearby rivers. Yet, crocodiles inhabit *"the Nile and other Asintie and African rivers; [are] of enormous voracity and strength, as well as fleetness in swimming"* (Bergman, 1991; Goodhugh & Taylor, 1943, p. 760). This may be one reason why Southern Christians, for example, have played with the idea that Jonah may have been swallowed by a lake sturgeon. "*Lake sturgeons have been described as primitive. They live up to 150 years, are capable of growing up to eight feet long, and weighing 300 pounds. They are stocked in Tennessee by the [Tennessee Wildlife Resources Agency] TWRA, and they travel great distances. They are considered to be endangered species in Tennessee, and therefore cannot be harvested*" (Tennessee Fishing Guide, 2016). "*Lake Sturgeon Certificates are issued to anglers who report the size of their catch, approximate weight, location, bait, and possible photograph fish, and release them to the wild*" (Tennessee Fishing Guide, 2016). Recognition from some states for documenting and aiding in the survival of the sturgeon may inspire fishermen to think about Jonah and the fish. Their thoughts may develop into cultural trends, for example sermons that influence their parishioners and their families. Christians tend to justify their beliefs with possibilities grounded in realism whereas Jewish tradition and culture may permit imaginative elaboration to demonstrate unlimited possibilities. *"The Talmudists represent leviathan to be a great fish, so great that one day it swallowed another fish which was nearly a thousand miles in extent. There were two, male and female, at first, but if they had both lived, the world would soon have been*" conquered (Goodhugh & Taylor, 1943, p. 760). "*[T]herefore the female was killed and laid up in salt for the great feast of the Messiah in the latter days"* (Goodhugh & Taylor, 1943, p. 760). Talmudist interpretations influence Christian scholars and ministers. Some Christians may interpret the great fish as a starfish, who later casts out Jonah; or as a squid, who holds and then releases Jonah. Some enormous tuna, grouper, and aquatic animals are capable of swallowing a whole human (Break Clips, 2014; Butler, 2016). Many Christians propose that *"Jonah says it's his fault,"* thus *"the sailors reluctantly throw him overboard"* (Finger, 2015, p. 37). *"Only entombment inside a 'great fish' will drive his bedraggled, stinking self to the city that needs to repent"* (Finger, 2015, p. 37). The allegory of entombment within a fish may be particularly interesting to Christians, who traditionally have funerary rituals involving the Earth, not the sea.

Christians may focus on entombment in this story. Jesus transcended death after three days, similarly to the story of Jonah, who should have died after being consumed. *"In 2014 the Islamic State destroyed the Mosul mosque in Iraq reputed to contain the tomb of the prophet Yunus"* known as Jonah to Christians (Jenkins, 2015, p. 36). *"Some Westerners saw this act as a blow against any surviving vestige of Christianity in the region, but of course Jonah is also venerated by Jews and Muslims"* (Jenkins, 2015, p. 36). "*Like many other patriarchs and prophets,"* Jonah "*is part of the common heritage of all three faiths, although these figures are imagined differently"* (Jenkins, 2015, p. 36). Christians may find that Muslim interpretations of Jonah's story also support the portrait of Jonah as a hero and a coward, who grows through God's grace. "*Similar mention is found in Koran 6:86. Finally, in Koran 68:48-50 there is another reference to Jonah only under the name of 'Man of the Fish*" (Steenbrink, 2002, p. 46). "*[B]e not like the Man of the Fish, when he cried out in agony. Had not grace from his Lord reached him, he would indeed have been cast off on the naked shore in disgrace. Thus did his Lord choose him and make him of the company of the righteous"* (Surah 68:48-50; Steenbrink, 2002, p. 46).

> *Save an old woman among those who stayed behind; Then We destroyed the others. And lo! ye verily pass by (the ruin of) them in the morning. And at night-time; have ye then no sense? And lo! Jonah verily was of those sent (to warn). When he ran away (like slave from captivity) to the ship (fully) laden. He (agreed to) cast lots, and he was condemned: Then the big Fish did swallow him, and he had done acts worthy of blame....And they believed; so We permitted them to enjoy (their life) for a while* (Surah 37:135-148).

> *Or is the Unseen theirs that they can write (thereof)? But wait thou for thy Lord's decree, and be not like him of the fish, who cried out in despair. Had it not been that [favor] from his Lord had reached him he surely had been cast into the wilderness while he was reprobate. But his Lord chose him and placed him among the righteous. And lo! those who disbelieve would fain disconcert thee with their eyes when they hear the Reminder, and they say: Lo! he is indeed mad* (Surah 68:47-51).

"[R]emember the Man of the Fish when he departed in wrath: he imagined that We had no power over him!" (Koran 21:87-88). Destruction of the tomb may seem disturbing to Christians, who commemorate Good Friday and Easter thereby reviving the importance of the tomb annually. *"Jewish sages, in contrast, stressed his frustration at being sent to save a gentile city, and they expanded his mission for messianic and apocalyptic ends. In the end times, they held, Jonah would slay the Leviathan who had swallowed him and serve it to God's faithful"* (Gregg, 2015; Jenkins, 2015, p. 36).

Life and death themes harmonize with themes of fertility present in Jesus' tale of life and death. *"Jonah stalks outside the city to sulk, though he is grateful for the bush that shades him from the sun. God sends a worm to attack the bush, and Jonah is truly ready to die"* (Finger, 2015, p. 39). Jonah dwells in misery. *"God has betrayed him by saving his worst enemies and killing his bush"* (Finger, 2015, p. 39). Christians are left to wonder about Jonah's outcome because God's retort is final. *"You cared about the life of one bush, Jonah. But should I not be concerned about a great city full of both repentant and innocent people? Should I not also care about the plight of animals?"* (Jonah 4:10-11). *"Before wrestling with the overall theology of this story, note unspoken issues of gender that balance the all-male human characters. The ship (feminine in Hebrew) takes on a female persona as she fears breaking up. Jonah lies asleep down in her hold"* (Finger, 2015, p. 39). *"[T]he feminine images of belly and womb within the ship, the fish, and in Sheol"* (i.e. the underworld) *"continue to both save"* and imprison *"Jonah in this wrestling match between Jonah and his God"* (Finger, 2015, p. 39). Jonah is a story about Jesus as much as about Jonah. Within Jonah's name there is a powerful allusion to Christ. *"Yonah in Hebrew means 'dove,' one of the birds used in very ancient sailing practice to guide lost sailors to land"* (*Judaism*, 1995, p. 344). *"According to a literal interpretation of his Hebrew name, Jonah is a 'dove' kept in the hold of the ship, something light and capable of flight. Yet, he engages in a downward"* flight when he is flung off the ship, sinks in the sea, and is ingested by the fish (*Judaism*, 1995, p. 344). Scholars may perceive that Jonah behaves like cargo. He may feel that to be a hero, he must surrender a personal power; and therefore demonstrates this surrender by behaving like an inert piece of property. *"Surely, he is stowed in the most dangerous place of the ship, among stones"* (*Judaism*, 1995, p. 344). Jonah behaves like a stone before being cast into the sea.

This story reinforces the message that *"Jonah in Christian typology"* is *"a figure of Jesus the [M]essiah"* (Jeffers, 2003, p. 62). *"The themes that appeared most often in early Christian visual art were Christ as the Good Shepherd, Jonah being regurgitated by leviathan (as a prefiguring of the Resurrection, Jonah appeared ten times more frequently than any other*

[B]iblical figure), and Noah and the Ark" (Woodworth, 2009). The commonly used motif demonstrates that Christians have enjoyed artfully interpreting Jonah's heroism and cowardice for centuries.

An artist's backstory may be essential for explaining why works explore Jewish themes (Baigell, 2013). For example, David Wander's *"spiritual journey"* is poignant because he used the tale of Jonah *"to visualize his own existential dilemmas and religious issues*" (Baigell, 2013, p. 12). Jonah "*became Wander's surrogate"* (Baigell, 2013, p. 12). *"[W]ondering what it meant to be Jewish," "he sought spiritual sustenance in eastern religions"* (Baigell, 2013, p. 12). A gentile "*suggested that he stop shopping the world's religions and turn to"* his own religion to find "*metaphysical"* truth (Baigell, 2013, p. 12). Jonah and the shipmen drew lots to determine culpability. Jonah admitted that his presence aboard the vessel precipitated the storm. He volunteered to be discarded overboard, and was swallowed whole by a great fish. A Jewish legend holds that the fish was aware of his or her impending death. The monstrous fish would have been killed and eaten by a leviathan; but, Jonah told the leviathan that he or she would be killed. The leviathan swam away; and Jonah remained inside the gigantic fish for three days. God commanded a female fish pregnant with 365,000 tiny babies in her belly to demand Jonah from the large fish. The pregnant fish threatened to swallow the host fish. Jonah entered the pregnant fish and resided with the fish's babies. Her womb was too crowded, so Jonah prayed to God to be exiled to Nineveh. The second fish spit out Jonah. After he announced their forthcoming destruction, the people repented and wore sack cloths. Wander finished *The Jonah Drawings,* a collection of sixteen drawings; and then illustrated five Scrolls: "*The Song of Songs, Ruth, Lamentations, Ecclesiastes, and Esther as well as the story of Joseph"* (Baigell, 2013, p. 12). *"At a little distance from the city, Jonah, looking depressed"* as Wander "*in effect proposing the following question" "running away from one's destiny," "and asking to die, as Jonah had asked....[T]he correct answer is to accept responsibility," "[c]onfronted"* by God, who "*created everything"* (Baigell, 2013, pp. 27-28). *"This is not merely any fish that swallows Jonah, it is a fish that has been designated for this task from the beginning of time"* (Zucker, 1995, pp. 365-368). The *Hero's Journey* made famous by Joseph Campbell (2008), is reaffirmed in Matthew 12:40: *"For as Jonah was three days and three nights in the belly of a huge fish, so the Son of Man will be three days and three nights in the heart of the earth"* (Northup, 2006). Jesus and Jonah share the hero's journey.

Jonah initially disavowed God's request to be a harbinger in sinful Nineveh. Over time, he experiences clarity and accepts God's command. He submits to forces beyond his control and becomes responsible for his actions. To distinguish right from wrong, he must comprehend that uncertainty cannot vanquish his hope and faith (Baigell, 2013). This is his heroic side. *"When in the belly of the great fish, Jonah comes to understand that the human condition is fraught with confusion and unanswered questions, but he must keep on keeping on"* (Baigell, 2013, p. 12). Here he is a coward; and yet, *"[f]utility is not an option. In short, Jonah has to do the best that he can do without quite knowing"* how, which is how he is cowardly because God told him exactly what to do before he got into the present situation (Baigell, 2013, p. 12). Wander felt a kindred spirit with Jonah because his *"existential dilemma reflected his own search for a moral anchor and ultimate"* truth (Baigell, 2013, p. 12). Cowardice is not *"knowing where one's actions will lead,"* despite having been informed of the exact course by God (Baigell, 2013, p. 12). The story Wander portrayed *"how to overcome the loneliness of being alone in the universe,"* and how envisioning Jonah as his partner *"allow[ed] his spirits to rise above nothingness, above the struggle with greed, avarice, and the baseness of life.... allow[ing] him the ability to maintain a sense of holiness in our day-to-day world"* (Baigell, 2013, p. 12-13). Disobedient heroes may overcome the karma of cowardice by *"never giving up"* (Baigell, 2013, p. 13). *"Jonah had no choice,"* which does not make him a hero, but a coward (Baigell, 2013, p. 13). However, he decided to make good choices when the opportunity presented itself, which is heroic, and ultimately is the legacy that he left. *"For Wander, this recapitulates both Jewish history and the history of everyman--when confused or beaten down, rise up"* to be a *"solitary individual"* (Baigell, 2013, p. 13). *"That is...both universal and personal"* (Baigell, 2013, p. 13). Heroism, therefore, is universal and personal, unlike cowardice, which is personal.

The Jonah Drawings, made in the late 1990s, suggest causation, but intently reveal personal tribulations. Wander haunts the audience with ink on watercolor paper. A massive 50-foot, 16-panel homage to pain, elucidation, and obedience spell out Jonah's feelings as experienced in Wander's heart. Three standalone paintings are accompanied by 13 images presented on two sections. The panels warn the audience about mythical possibilities and the presence of lore affecting humankind. The drawings promise silver linings for humanity's humble suffering, but scoff at mortality as a remnant of fear. The sea's desire to destroy; refrain from destroying; confession about having the power to destroy; and ungranted request to destroy humans (e.g. Jonah) is symbolized by four-cornered shapes. Humans' willingness to die for plants is mocked by Wander, who paints humans as being ignorant to their own frailty. Jonah's confidence in his mission is evident because he penetrates the depths, but his hesitation swallows him before the great fish eats him. "*In the panels directly relating to Jonah's experiences, Wander often places his hero close to the picture surface as if to emphasize the human drama of the scene"* (Baigell, 2013, p. 13). Viewers *"are meant to concern"* themselves *"with Jonah's personal dilemmas and to empathize with his difficulties in making decisions"* (Baigell, 2013, p. 13). The metaphor of Wander/Jonah is disconnected because Wander knows that in retrospect Jonah chooses to let evil be dominant (Baigell, 2013). In Wander's idea of Jonah, he flees and take to the high seas where Jonah interprets himself *"as a positive sign"* (Baigell, 2013, p. 24). *"Thus he was taught the lesson that God is Lord over heaven and earth and sea, and man cannot hide himself from His face"* (Baigell, 2013, p. 25). Even when doing the right thing is easy, one may not hide.

After he surrendered to God and was swallowed by the fish, Jonah may have felt joy, relief, or pleasure. Transforming dreaded tasks into opportunities for fun and personal satisfaction are evident in Fish Philosophy. Fish Philosophy is about making work what you make of it. *"Sometimes it is quite marvelous and sometimes it is like visiting the prison population"* (Lundin, et al., 2002, p. 2). *"It is the lighthearted feeling you release inside people when they are enthused, committed, and free of fear"* (Lundin, et al., 2002, p. 11). Fish philosophy is an ethos generated by fishmongers, who invite customers to transform commerce into playtime. *"Play must come from within and so you can only invite play"* (Lundin, et al., 2002, p. 11). *"Play also requires trust"* (Lundin, et al., 2002, p. 12). *"Playfulness won't flourish in places where people spend more time trying not to do the wrong thing than they do searching for ways to do the right thing"* (Lundin, et al., 2002, p. 12). *"[P]eople often master the job so quickly that it can become almost second nature"* (Lundin, et al., 2002, p. 15). *"[I]n a job that could easily have become repetitious and predictable,...fishmongers chose to make it fun and always surprising"* (Lundin, et al., 2002, p. 19). *"[N]ow [they] try to find opportunities to play or be there, instead of demanding automatic responses that may not always be appropriate"* (Lundin, et al., 2002, p. 28.) *"But as our culture changed, people became happier, upbeat, [and] relaxed...I know it's not normal anymore...[to] deal with [these] issue[s] immediately, which just means...[the] workplace is going to be better"* (Lundin, et al., 2002, p. 34). *"Today...[participants] also play a major role in identifying opportunities for better performance"* (Lundin, et al., 2002, p. 30). Professionals at Sprint have created a similarly candid and fun atmosphere. *"The Pond,"* a place for reconciliation, *"is for when you need to have a conversation with someone....Maybe someone stepped on your toes, or you think they're not listening to you, or they're doing something that's not consistent with our vision of being world famous....There are no rules in the Pond, except to be respectful"* (Lundin, et al., 2002, p. 128). *"[O]nce you do it, it feels so good. I have yet to be in a position where I've poured out my heart and not gotten a good response"* (Lundin, et al., 2002, p. 129). Fish Philosophy is a transformative tool that reflects Christians' dual aspects, for example death and rebirth.

Christians may have fun by guessing at and amusing themselves with the concept of which animal may possibly have participated in God's scheme to command Jonah to warn Nineveh. Christians know that any animal could have answered God's call. Thus, the question is irrelevant. However, the meaning of the story is amplified by these analyses, which draw attention to variability present in this tale. The truth of the story is embedded in the dual role of hero and coward. Jonah's recycling of attitudes throughout makes the reader believe that he is either at any point.

Chapter 2

Jesus and the 12 disciples

The Bible's *"fishing motif has traditionally been regarded as a kind of recruiting slogan"* (Stendahl, 1998, p. 79). Though some Christians *"confess to thinking that Jesus could have done better"* in terms of redundancy, notwithstanding *"its ghastly ironies, the U.S. Army's invitation to 'Be all you can be' has a lot more going for it"* (Stendahl, 1998, p. 79). Military gusto is a fundamental aspect American national self-esteem presently—and has been for many decades since the Good War (Northup, 2008). What does it mean to "be all you can be" or to "be a fisher of men?" *"Perhaps its very ambiguity is part of the hook. Perhaps the disciples left their nets precisely because they wanted to find out what these words meant. It may be that it is curiosity as much as any reward or understood promise that draws people down the...road"* (Stendahl, 1998, p. 79). Perchance these institutions offer what *"especially seemed to Americans"* to be *"really a promise about success"* (Stendahl, 1998, p. 79). *"[D]rawing in netloads"* of people (Stendahl, 1998, p. 79). The iconic message is a *"selling point," "a promise"; "quite literally," "attractiveness" "to become one of those who would make so great and growing a company from a small band"* (Stendahl, 1998, p. 79). *"Simon and his mates will pull the nets for the great apocalyptic catch, they will sit to cull the bad from the good, they will be like the angels or the courtiers of God's kingdom rather than part of the teeming masses to be judged"* (Stendahl, 1998, p. 79). *"[P]robably most appealing"* is that *"the imagery may speak of that work which gathers and connects, which binds in networks of new and unsought relationships"* (Stendahl, 1998, p. 79). *"The intuitive group also began their presentation by drawing"* awareness *"adopted for dealing with the task" "[t]hey had approached....The disciples trusted Jesus to deal with the crowd"* (Moroz, 2011). *"They ha[d] been among the villages of Galilee (9:1), at Bethsaida for the multiplication of loaves and fish"* (O'Brien, 2008). "*Once again,"* Christians *"might add that God always finds" "the kingdom as something marvelous and wonderful"* (O'Brien, 2008). God *"will give up everything else to have it[; b]ut what of those who find that living the kingdom of heaven can often appear ambiguous and confusing, full of difficult decisions"* (O'Brien, 2008)*?* The "*parable can be seen to respond to them by portraying the painstaking work of fishermen who must sift carefully through their catch and separate what they judge to be good fish from those that are* *of no use"* (O'Brien, 2008). However, their *"painstaking work"* is recompensed with fish to bring home (O'Brien, 2008). *"The value of this seemingly ordinary and even arduous living of the kingdom is emphasized by the way Jesus says that it mirrors the work of the angels at the end of time"* (O'Brien, 2008). *"They will take great care to ensure that the good are singled out and only the wicked thrown away. Are [Christians] more likely to do so and turn to God when things are tough"* (O'Brien, 2008)*?*

"'Catching people' may be a powerful description of what Simon will be doing, but it is not what captures him" (Stendahl, 1998, p. 79). *"The church's nets are often ripped by the strain of so many live fish"* (Stendahl, 1998, p. 79). *"What engages Simon is not a recruitment slogan;" "the meaning of Jesus' words has short-circuited the narrative"* (Stendahl, 1998, p. 79). Yet, *"the net did not burst;"* but, *"so often dualistic"* Christians *"picture[] the net as elastic and strong"* (Stendahl, 1998, p. 79). *"Luke does not give us a story of Jesus walking the shore to recruit his disciples with imperative or ambiguous words of call"* (Stendahl, 1998, p. 79). The story describing a great storm contextualizes Jesus as a fisher of men, meaning a soul seeker. *"Luke's story about the beginning of discipleship is not a story about calling but a story about fishing"* (Stendahl, 1998, p. 79). Stories about fishing *"are usually stories of prodigious surprise, of unlikely triumphs,"* and incredible confrontations with *"elusive glory"* (Stendahl, 1998, p. 79). *"To fish"* requires a fisher *"to depend on the unseen"* and have faith about *"what is hidden in the waters"* (Stendahl, 1998, p. 79). Strangely, some fish seem to *"disappear, and sometimes the mysterious sea delivers up its bounty"* (Stendahl, 1998, p. 79). A *"consistent failure in attempts to catch fish"* may prompt a thinker not to believe in *"operation of ordinary luck,"* but *"instead [that] it [is]...fate"* causing *"catchlessness"* (Stendahl, 1998, p. 79). *"This distinction"* may illustrate to *"the playful imagination that there might be an even higher or deeper determination, a destiny surprising and sweet enough to overturn...fate"* (Stendahl, 1998, p. 79). Fishers depending on fish to make ends meet, understand the *"contingency and fragility of life and fortune"* (Stendahl, 1998, p. 79). *"Luke 5 is another fishing story about an amazing catch,"* yet it correlates *"good fortune"* with *"humility"* and blessings with a *"sense of unworthiness. The fish story thus becomes not about luck, but about blessing. It becomes personal" "to translate ordinary fortune into humbling wonder"* and *"privilege"* (Stendahl, 1998, p. 79). Calling is intricately woven into the mission of following and catching (Troyer, 2010). *"The primary purpose" "is seen in the first callings....as portrayed in the call of the first disciples"* (Troyer, 2010, p. 11). The new disciples are portrayed as being *"part of the apocalyptic plan of Jesus...calling...four [fishermen]...for two distinct purposes"* (Troyer, 2010, p. 11). One is to follow and the other is to *"become*

'fishers of men'" (Troyer, 2010, p. 11). In Mark, *"Jesus has in mind a joining of...presence and practice[, which] illustrate the participation of the disciples"* (Troyer, 2010, p. 11). This *"[implies] a radical break with their former way"* of *"earning a living....Instead of living by the fishing business, they will live to reach others"* (Troyer, 2010, p. 11). Mark suggests *"with an affirmation on the purpose"* of calling that the disciples were called to serve God, not to fish souls or fish (Troyer, 2010, p. 12). *"[T]o participate in the work of Jesus" is "[t]he second purpose"* (Troyer, 2010, p. 12). *"[I]n the episode involving Levi (Mark 2:17)....a look into the purpose of calling is revealed"* (Troyer, 2010, p. 12). *"[E]vents surrounding the call unfold"* (Troyer, 2010, p. 12). The *"narrative with Levi"* exhibits *"Jesus call...[to] someone...not in high standing with the community"* (Troyer, 2010, p. 12). *"The fact that Levi is a tax collector would cause those around Jesus to possibly feel"* disdain for his profession and possibly *"confused or anxious at such a choice"* (Troyer, 2010, p. 12). *"Mark shows that Jesus came to call sinners"* (Mark 1-8:26; Troyer, 2010, p. 12). *"Following Jesus" "is a key component. Included in the endeavor"* is the meaning of life (Troyer, 2010, p. 12). *"Making the choice to follow a leader"* is necessary today as it was in Jesus' era (Troyer, 2010, p. 12). *"Purpose and mission"* are *"key"* (Troyer, 2010, p. 12). This point would have followed from the Old Testament. *"This relationship is expressed in the obedience to the call of a military leader to follow into battle. Two instances that reinforce this concept of following are found in the mission of"* Judges 9:9 and I Samuel 11:6 (Troyer, 2010, p. 12). The occurrence in I Samuel 11:6 particularly illustrates *"a call to action"* (Troyer, 2010, p. 12). *"As the"* verse *"revolves around"* a *"siege,"* the *"call to action, dedication[,] and commitment would have led to a following battle"* (Troyer, 2010, p. 12). *"The circumstances"* create a need for a *"leader for a great cause,"* who does not mind the *"personal cost"* (Troyer, 2010, p. 12). *"A further"* depiction *"of following a leader in a time of importance is seen in the time of the Maccabaean revolt. A charismatic leader of those who chose to"* enter *"the covenant of their fathers" "led a revolt against the atrocities being committed against the temple and the people"* (Troyer, 2010, p. 14). *"After reaching the limit of tolerance," "Mattathias proclaimed his mission and summoned his followers"* (Troyer, 2010, p. 14). They *"cried throughout the city with a loud voice, saying, whosoever is zealous of the law...let him follow me. So he and his sons fled into the mountains, and left all that ever they had in the city"* (1 Maccabees 2:27-28). These measures demonstrate the relationship between leaders and followers during a critical time. *"The leader is portrayed as one calling people to himself" "along with the sacrifice and allegiance of the followers. The followers show allegiance to their leader,"* and what *"it meant to be a follower. The first disciples would have been aware of a basic concept"* (Troyer, 2010, p. 14).

Subordination is important because observation and emulation of the teacher are necessary (Troyer, 2010). Mark demonstrates Jesus' intention in *"spiritual authority"* (Troyer, 2010, p. 16). Mark's rendition of the disciples following Jesus is distinct because their transformation transpired apart from a student-teacher relationship. Because Jesus was in command, he selected the followers he desired. *"A further aspect to consider of the initial call narratives that appear in the beginning of the gospel is the identification of the person who takes initiative to commence the call"* (Troyer, 2010, p. 17). In Mark, Jesus is "*the one who calls"* a desired subordinate. Jesus glorifies the act and purpose of calling. Calling is an activity that Jesus initiates and demonstrates. Jesus is "*appointed*" to go his own "*way,*" and he desires specific followers, so he instigates a call to action and directs his follower to learn how to call by following him (Troyer, 2010, p. 17). "*Jesus is the one who sees and calls"* (Troyer, 2010, p. 17).

God offers insight about how to answer Jesus' call. "*The positive and negative judgments"* may be evaluated *"next to each other"* (Troyer, 2010, p. 10). Yet, a call is a powerful beacon and the choice to answer is symbolic, not practicable. Answer equates with following, which is fundamental to discipleship. This "*specific mode of following is not necessarily universal in nature among all who choose to follow. This is observed in the previously discussed callings and subsequent"* callings *"as they are similar in nature"* (Troyer, 2010, p. 20). "*The type and nature of calling and following as recorded by Mark vary"* (Troyer, 2010, p. 20). *"They do not all appear to be identical and therefore imply that the calling of Jesus and the response to Jesus"* may vary between followers (Troyer, 2010, p. 20).

The disciples characterize Jesus differently by demonstrating separate reactions to his call, but Mark shows openness allowing for diversity (Troyer, 2010). Mark's interpretation does not abridge otherness, but makes room for differences. For example, Mark's records depict how Simon and Andrew answered their call to follow. They reacted similarly by deserting fishing and following Jesus (Mark 1:18). Putting aside and following are two separate actions. In the next description, Mark says that they leave others behind. Simon and Andrew abandoned their families, which is different than deserting an occupation and professional equipment (Mark: 1:20; Troyer, 2010, p. 20). The scene is set by the idea of fishermen going to fish. Immediately the audience's attention is drawn by the narrative to tools of the trade. *"This tips the balance, since boat, nets, and fish figure more prominently and relevantly in the scene leading up to the Jesus [scene]"* (Wiarda, 2004, p. 182). "*If Jesus' words do refer to fish and fishing, they confirm a causal connection....[and] reinforce the view that the dialogue [serves] as love's active demonstration"* (Wiarda, 2004, p. 182). It *"has been proven by the Holy Bible teachings that reaching out to communities will open doors to teach the world"* (Martin, 2014). For example, the *"parable of the mustard seed"* crosses several barriers (Podgurski & Writer, 2004). *"With a selection of Easter Bible readings,"* a teacher could tell *"them about the empty tomb, the story of Jesus meeting his followers on the road to Emmaus, and of Jesus eating the fish with his disciples on the Sea of Galilee"* (Danbury, 2016). Therefore, disciples are given the choice to be one of Jesus' followers, but are not obligated to do so.

Post-resurrection Jesus appeared before his disciples became aware that he was present (Hoehl, 2008; John 21:1-25). He commands them to toss their fishing net to the right side of the boat. When it lands, they catch many fish and finally recognize the man on the shore, Jesus. His disciples are invited to eat breakfast, fish. *"The differences between Mark and Matthew are slight here. Matthew says Jesus was walking about alongside the Sea, Mark that he was going along by it"* (Duncan & Derret, 1980, p. 110). *"They were not unemployed or poor persons who wanted some fish, the readily-available diet of poor and rich alike, but were fishermen by occupation. Jesus, without preliminaries, orders them to follow him, i.e. to be his disciples, 'and I shall cause you to be fishers of men'"* (Duncan & Derret, 1980, p. 110). Similar to the miraculous catch, feeding of the multitude suggests abundance. *"None of the three synoptics suggests any hesitation on the chosen men's part. 'They immediately left the nets and followed him (i.e. accepted the role of students of his).' He went on and saw James and John...(the men who will eventually debate the power-structure of the church)"* (Duncan & Derret, 1980, p. 110). The narrative appears to be perfunctory, but the audience's interest soon becomes satisfied. A hungry mass of people unexpectedly receives an unlimited portion of free fish and bread. Conflict shifts from a congregation of hungry people to the wildness of a group ravishing free delicacies. The conflict is resolved when disciples and audience members accept that Jesus maintained control. Satisfaction correlates with Jesus' control over the situation because the crowd could have been dissatisfied (e.g. overindulgent). Jesus again demonstrates that following him requires service. On this occasion, disciples served the multitudes by distributing loaves and fishes. *"Realizing the incomprehension of the disciples, every one ate and was satisfied"* (Cai, 2011, p. 121). Judas may have asked whether they could afford to feed the multitude demonstrating his lack of faith (Camille, 2001; Forbes, 2010). *"Jesus took the loaves, gave thanks, and shared the loaves[, which causes Christians]...to [recognize] the abundance of God's love and of God's generosity. God has enough to feed us practically, physically and spiritually"* (Francis, 2012).

Jesus commanded the multitudes. *"Jesus gave them simple ministry tasks, such as finding food and preparing for the Passover meal"* (Francis, 2012). His *"disciples know him as they eat his broiled fish; the...disciples recognize him in the breaking of bread"* (Gittins, 1994). Jesus is *"the true protagonist...; [a]lmost all the actions and words come from him: greeting, questions, reproach, order, revelation of his hands and feet, even asking for something to eat and eating it in front of them. Except for offering him a piece of fish, the disciples' role is limited to listening in silence"* (Pérez Herrero, 2006). Perhaps they reconstructed tales about fish to make sense of why Jesus had emphasized fish so severely. For example, *"the only sign given to the rebellious generation will be the sign of Jonah's three days in the belly of the fish (12:40)....Jonah's three days and nights in the fish and his application to the death and resurrection of Jesus"* (Douglas, 2009, pp. 141-142). *"On the other hand, Jesus' body still bears the marks of his crucifixion; there is no denying who he is. Thomas can touch him (20:25-27), and Jesus can eat fish with Peter and...other disciples"* (Reddit, 2007). Their calling determined their destinies in two ways: first they were called to be all they could be; and second, they were asked to determine what that would be based on Jesus' emphasis on fish. This application is evident today in the Army's slogan "be all you can be," which leaves one's achievement open to discretion and interpretation.

Chapter 3

Five loaves and two fish

Animal welfare has been promoted in contemporary culture. Throughout modern history, animals primarily have been portrayed by the media as workers and pets. A paradigmatic shifts to include animals as victims has been documented and advanced by reality television shows (Moore, 2011). This shift is especially evident in depictions of fish. For example, during the 1960s, the television show *Flipper* portrayed a bottlenose dolphin, who protected marine life, caught criminals, and rescued people (Cowden, 1964). Reality television shows, such as *Sea Shepherds* and *Alaskan State Trooper*, depict humane treatment of animals. Marine life, including reefs, mammal, birds, and other forms are guarded, regulated, conserved, and protected (Baum, 2014). Although television shows depict agentic narratives in which officers and volunteers protect fishing industries' interests, many shows attempt to appeal to audiences and impact their attitudes towards fish by depicting stewardship. Television shows appeal to a "*dual audience*," who want industry to thrive and want to conserve fish (Scott, 2016). Christians' desires to protect marine life and to reframe popular conceptions of fish may be relate to the story of the loaves and fishes (John 6:1-58; Luke 9:10-17; Mark 6:30-52; Mark 8:1-21; Matthew 14:13-33; Matthew 16:5-12). Jesus, "*the dual-identity avenger-vigilante*," multiplies the number of fish and loaves to feed the multitudes (Coogan, 2016). Jesus attempts to transform their meaning and value. Fish are valuable commodities. Jesus lowers their value by creating abundance. Jesus may use several devices, such as analogies and persuasion, to demonstrate that living fish are distinguishable from dead fish. His methods are indirect, yet clearly communicate a message.

Dual narratives have been used for millenniums to convey heroism, which is elucidated by this story. He is like modern-day superheroes, including reality television stars. "*One can identify the three primary conventions of the superhero genre. The most identifiable element" "is that the protagonist has superpowers—extraordinary abilities, advanced technology, or highly developed physical and/or mental skills (including mystical abilities)*" (Coogan, 2016). Next, "*the superhero has a selfless, pro-social mission, which means that his fight against evil must fit in with the existing, professed mores of society and must not be intended to benefit or further himself*" (Coogan, 2016). Lastly, *"the protagonist has a specific superhero identity, which is embodied in a codename and iconic costume,"* expressive of "*the superhero's biography, inner character, powers, or origin—the transformation from ordinary person to superhero"* (Coogan, 2016). Typical *"superheroes have dual identities, the ordinary one of which is usually a closely guarded secret. The identity element comprises the codename and the costume, with the secret identity being a customary counterpart to the codename. The identity convention most clearly marks the superhero as different from his predecessors"* (Coogan, 2016). Jesus meets the three criteria: 1) he has the power to multiply fish and resurrect from the dead; 2) he helps the poor and hungry; and 3) his public identity was of a carpenter and rabbi, but his secret identity was the immaculately conceived Son of God (Mark 6:3). Jesus differed from other prophets because he taught salvation. "*Superheroic identities externalize either their alter ego's inner character or biography"* (Coogan, 2016). The chief conventions "*—mission, powers, and identity—"* define the genre's fundament. "*The similarities between specific instances of a genre are semantic, abstract, and thematic, and come from the constellation of conventions*" that are nearly always evident in superhero stories (Coogan, 2016). *"If a character basically fits the mission-powers-identity definition, even with significant qualifications, and cannot be easily placed into another genre because of the preponderance of superhero-genre conventions, the character is a superhero"* (Coogan, 2016). Jesus fits *"the dual-identity avenger-vigilante"* profile because he miraculously multiplies fish to feed the hungry multitudes (Coogan, 2016). His 40 day fast is closely linked with the story of the multitudes because in both stories Jesus considers producing bread. His two-fold identity of savior and carpenter is manifested because he defends against hunger without fishing.

"There are multiple themes in the story lines, including transformation and identity," to appeal to the *"dual audience"* (Dong, 2006; Scott, 2016). *"Nonetheless, in pitting the two groups against one another, the show presents a duality"* (Ehrenhalt & Prachi, 2016). *"[T]hrough the dual strains of destiny and choice"* heroes emerge (DiMare, 2011, p. 237). Jesus' conscientiousness toward fish is revitalized (Baum, 2014). The two dominant depictions are both recognized as being sacred. The first is sacred because humans have likely always fished, and fishing persists as one of the world's greatest markets. It maintains cultural heritage, local economies, and globalized industries. Fish are a staple throughout the world. The second demonstrates that humans may have a responsibility to protect animals, which is sacred. On television, profanation of the sacred and discrete realms indicates villainy. For example, fishermen, who illegally trap crabs are exposed, shamed, and fined. One suspect had 12 illegal crab pots. "*It's just a killing machine at the bottom of the ocean"* (Baum, 2014). "*[T]hat's a grand*

total of $120,000 in fines" (Baum, 2014). *"Because of this guy's past history, he's going to be looking at possibly the loss of his fishing privileges for some time. In this case it was a good day. We caught a suspect, who really has no regard for the regulations or resources"* (Baum, 2014). *"It's becoming a waste issue, a conservation issue. So, it was a good day. We seized 12 pots. Hopefully we can get good fines and outcomes in this case"* (Baum, 2014). Heroes prevent *"killing [of] innocent animals in a world where it doesn't belong anymore"* (*Whale Wars*, 2008). For example, a television show depicts vigilantes attacking ships that savagely hunt whales. The show depicts international shame associated with hunting elusive marine mammals. Laurens de Groot, a Netherlands Deckhand, said *"That ship stands for everything I hate"* (*Whale Wars*, 2008). Captain Paul Watson said, *"[t]he Nisshin Maru...is the largest whale killing machine on the planet"* (*Whale Wars*, 2008). Fishing vessels that transport dead fish to ports are regulated and assisted when they encounter difficulty on the ocean, for example in shows such as *Coast Guard Alaska* (Roker & Muth, 2011).

The miracle of Jesus feeding the multitudes by multiplying the loaves and fish is described in all four Gospels of the New Testament (Sick, 2015). Jesus attempts to change the way that his disciples view fish. He weaves together several lessons. He feeds the needy; he collects the remains; and he walks on water. By walking on water after feeding the multitudes, Jesus avoided travelling on a fishing boat. While on the Sea of Galilee, he may have performed a ceremony to reconcile with fish. He may have replenished the fish (Schaefer & Savulescu, 2014). Jesus may not have needed to replenish the fish. He may have created flesh, but not souls. He may have multiplied dead fish. He also identified and distinguished dead fish as an asset by collecting scraps to feed the needy. This distinction is essential because his disciples act as fishermen, but Jesus does not fish.

Jesus is not tempted by fish. This is evident in his taste for bread. Jesus does not discuss eating fish; however, he often discusses eating bread. For example, in John 6:5 Jesus asked Philip where they could buy bread to feed the multitude. While Jesus was fasting he is tempted by Satan, who suggested that Jesus should turn stones into bread. The average person living during his era may have been more tempted by fish than bread. Although Satan likely knew that Jesus could create bread and fish, Satan only tempted Jesus with bread. Jesus does not want to change the custom of dining and feasting by abruptly altering the traditional menu when he feeds the multitude. He wants to be a hero for the hungry and expressed compassion towards fish. Docetists may envision that he expresses conflicted feelings in the form of riddles and analogy.

> *The next day, the crowd that had remained on the other side of the sea realized that only one boat had been there, and that Jesus had not boarded it with His disciples, but they had gone away alone. However, some boats from Tiberias arrived near the place they had eaten the bread after the Lord had given thanks. So when the crowd saw that neither Jesus nor His disciples were there, they got into the boats and went to Capernaum to look for Him. When they found Him on the other side of the sea, they asked Him, "Rabbi, when did You get here?" Jesus replied, "Truly, truly, I tell you, it is not because you saw these signs that you are looking for Me, but because you ate the loaves and had your fill*
> (John 6: 22-26).

Jesus reminds the multitude how filling bread was. He also extolls them not to eat food that can be killed.

> *'Do not work for food that perishes, but for food that endures to eternal life, which the Son of Man will give you. For God the Father has placed His seal of approval on Him.' Then they inquired, 'What must we do to perform the works of God?' Jesus replied, 'This is the work of God: to believe in the One He has sent.' So they asked Him, 'What sign then will You perform, so that we may see it and believe You? What will You do?'*
> (John 6: 27-30).

Jesus approves of their inquisitiveness about his riddle. He replies by offering another riddle. *"Our fathers ate the manna in the wilderness, as it is written: 'He gave them bread from heaven to eat* (John 6: 31).*'"* Jesus said to them, *"Truly, truly, I tell you, it was not Moses who gave you the bread from heaven, but it is My Father who gives you the true bread from heaven"* (John 6: 32). Jesus reframes his answer by alluding to the Jews' religion. *"For the bread of God is He who comes down from heaven and gives life to the world"* (John 6: 32). Jesus conquers their imaginations. They say, *"Sir,...give us this bread at all times"* (John 6:34). He offers them unlimited bread. *"Jesus answered, 'I am the bread of life. Whoever comes to Me will never hunger, and whoever believes in Me will never thirst'"* (John 6:35). He analogizes bread with unlimited wine, a miracle for which he may have been well known (John 6:36). *"But as I told you, you have seen Me and still you do not believe. All that the Father gives Me will come to Me, and the one who comes to Me I will never turn away"* (John 6:36-37). Jesus references religion again to pique their interest.

> *'For I have come down from heaven, not to do My own will, but to do the will of Him who sent Me. And this is the will of Him who sent Me, that I shall lose none of all those He has given Me, but raise them up at the last day. For it is My Father's will that everyone who looks to the Son and believes in Him shall have eternal life, and I will raise him up at the last day.' At this, the Jews began to grumble about Jesus because He had said, 'I am the bread that came down from heaven'* (John 6:38-41).

He may have suggested that raised souls are like bread. Jesus attempted to negotiate the terms and meaning of fish, but he was outmatched by their greed. *"They were asking, 'Is this not Jesus, the son of Joseph, whose father and mother we know? How then can He say, 'I have come down from heaven?""* (John 6:42). He admonishes them.

> *'Stop grumbling among yourselves,' Jesus replied. 'No one can come to Me unless the Father who sent Me draws him, and I will raise him up at the last day. It is written in the prophets: 'And they will all be taught by God.' Everyone who has heard the Father and learned from Him comes to Me—not that anyone has seen the Father except the One who is from God; only He has seen the Father'* (John 6:43-46).

Jesus attempted to mix metaphors by referencing fishing nets. *"Truly, truly, I tell you, he who believes has eternal life"* (John 6:47). *"Of course, as [Christians] know from Christ's"* message *"all animals, even fish of the sea, are those that lead us to the kingdom of heaven"* (Hannah, 2006, p. 52).

Jesus returns to his sticking point.

> *I am the bread of life. Your fathers ate the manna in the wilderness, yet they died. This is the bread that comes down from heaven so that anyone may eat of it and not die. I am the living bread that came down from heaven. If anyone eats of this bread, he will live forever. And this bread, which I will give for the life of the world, is My flesh* (John 6:48-51).

He created chaos to regain control over the conversation.

> *At this, the Jews began to argue among themselves, 'How can this man give us His flesh to eat?' So Jesus said to them, 'Truly, truly, I tell you, unless you eat the flesh and drink the blood of the Son of Man, you have no life in you. Whoever eats My flesh and drinks My blood has eternal life, and I will raise him up at the last day. For My flesh is real food, and My blood is real drink. Whoever eats My flesh and drinks My blood remains in Me, and I in him. Just as the living Father sent Me and I live because of the Father, so also the one who feeds on Me will live because of Me. This is the bread that came down from heaven. Unlike your fathers, who ate the manna and died, the one who eats this bread will live forever'* (John 6:52-58).

Jesus won the debate. Understanding their desire to eat bodies, he analogized bread to bodies perhaps in hopes of satisfying them. *"Through the use of bread as a symbol John has focused first on the saving efficacy of belief in Jesus and then drawn out the saving efficacy of his death....Only those who come to believe in him and his saving death find the fulfillment of their quest for life"* (Green, McKnight, & Marshall, 1992, p. 86). Finally, Jesus eats broiled fish after his resurrection (Easton, 2005, p. 260; Matthew 14:19).

Chapter 4

Noah's ark

The flood and Noah's ark were a special *"opportunity to provide" "education to"* such *"large numbers"* (Keulartz, 2015, p. 342). Yet, Noah's story is a tragedy. It is not a celebratory tale as explained by many Christian scholars. God's primary mission in the story is to inform Noah that unless he builds the ark, he and his family will die. Noah is not a hero, although he is a protagonist. He is a servant.

A zoo's job is to protect animals. They are not heroic. Like Noah, a zoo is a servant to human society in order to captivate them with the majesty of biodiversity. Similarly to the tale of Noah and the ark, *"[i]n the latest strategy, the primary mission of zoos is to integrate all…elements with their efforts to protect endangered species and conserve healthy ecosystems"* (Keulartz, 2015, p. 342). *"Education in the context of the integrated approach must be fully geared,….but it seems that two courses of action are absolutely essential to achieve the desired effect"* (Keulartz, 2015, p. 342). The first is *"conventionalist"* because Noah just built an ark to contain all the wildlife (Keulartz, 2015, p. 338). The second is traditionalist because Noah must rely on God. In the zoo, different kinds of animals flourish, but they have no plan, such as a Species Survival Plan. They are like Noah's family. For example, a white tiger may flourish without human populations admiring the exhibit; however, they need human intervention to survive in captivity. Similarly, Noah's family could have survived if they would have had faith in God, but they needed Noah to have faith in God for them. He was the first to have faith in God, and then they followed him and were saved because he had faith in God. In Islamic narratives, Noah may have only boarded two of every kind of his animals; however the Christian perspective is that Noah boarded two of every kind of animal on the planet—which is impossible given the size of his boat. Two of every kind of his animals is a more reasonable assessment of the quantity of animals saved. However, scholars do not know what kind of animals Noah had. That information cannot be presumed based on Biblical truths about who had which kinds of animals at that time because Noah may have been an atypical steward. He may have had white tigers, for example, because they roamed in India, which was near his home.

Noah is not a savior, who protects animals, he protected humans because he was a servant and a humble family man. The Noahide laws, developed from this lesson to teach people how not to kill themselves or other living beings, including any living insect no matter how big or little, may be used to explain the origins of water on Earth. Noah's tale ends when all the fish fear him. "*For many years (already in ancient Greece and creeping into the English language) it was*" recognized *"that water had a role to play in the subtle area of mind, where water was given various names depending on the way that it manifested"* (Dickens, 2000, p. 258). *"Humors,"* as they were known, have the "*essence*" of water or vapor (Dickens, 2000, p. 258) *"Humor"* bears an etymological relationship with "*humidity*" (Dickens, 2000, p. 258). *"Four [humors] were identified and were thought to determine the physical and mental well being by their mixture. An attempt has been made to fit the guna to these"* humors (Dickens, 2000, p. 258). *"Noah had it easy. All he had to do was collect two of everything. Today's Noahs now have to [decide] which species make it into the ark that will deliver them safely to the future"* (*The Futurist,* 1995, p. 40). *"The difference between the [B]iblical Noah and today's is that"* selective decisions *"will not make everyone happy, but making these tough choices is our"* duty. Poor choices result in *"globalization"* that *"causes massive dislocations of entire populations"* (Keulartz, 2015, p. 336).

The *"Noah's Ark Problem"* uses an *"allegory"* to extract *"a vivid image of the core problem," "maximizing diversity"* with a constrained budget (Weitzman, 1998, p. 1285). It envisions a decision-making model in which points are assigned based on ranked factors. For example, the specialness and beauty of a white tiger, and the fact that they draw paying crowds to zoos, may be worth more than lack of abundance (Cusack, 2016). *"[A]bove all"* an *"interventionist strategy"* is *"unavoidable"* (Keulartz, 2015, p. 336). *"[A]nimal ethicists demonstrate [Noah's] 'ecological illiteracy'"* by assessing the *"moral worth"* of conservation habitats (Keulartz, 2015, p. 338). *"Another potential area...between wildlife conservationists and animal activists concerns managed relocation (also known as assisted colonization or assisted migration). The human-aided relocation....where environmental conditions are more suitable is impossible"* (Keulartz, 2015, p. 336). *"[T]he Noah's Ark paradigm...has lost credibility and has gradually given way to a new paradigm: the 'integrated approach'....[T]he zoo is primarily seen as a conservation park...in the best possible way...[with maximum] species conservation benefits"* (Keulartz, 2015, p. 337). *"In this scheme of things the zoo[s],"* and *"accompanying loss of biodiversity, began to turn their attention to the conservation of endangered species and wildlife"* (Keulartz, 2015, p. 337). Under either model, *"modern zoos must commit to the conservation of species and wildlife"* (Keulartz, 2015, p. 337). The *"Noah's Ark metaphor [is] intended to portray a situation where not only are [Earthlings] saved from a disastrous flood, but it is possible to maintain the integrity of a unifying framework"* (Smith & Pattanayak, 2002, p. 290). *"Noah's ark is the only ark described by the Bible, but may not have been the only ark that God commanded to be built"* (Rehmann, 2000). Perhaps zoos and aquariums are arks commanded by God to be built.

U.S. zoos and aquariums have *"a strong mission focus....Most zoos and aquariums are vital economic generators. One of the great misperceptions of zoos and aquariums is that they can be a modern day Noah's Ark"* (Coan, 2015, p. 284). Neither zoos, nor aquariums can possibly accommodate all of the helpless animals. *"Global biodiversity is currently suffering one of the largest and swiftest mass"* suffering of species *"events ever. Potentially great risks to human well-being; loss of potential resources for agriculture, medicine, industry, and culture; as well as ethical issues are involved"* (Lev-Yadun, 2009, p. 174). *"Such solutions as sustainable management, restoration of damaged ecosystems, and conservation in small reserves or in botanical and zoological gardens will"* help some animals, but not all (Lev-Yadun, 2009, p. 174). Humans *"cannot just sit by and watch the treasures of biodiversity disappear and do so little to reduce the damage"* (Lev-Yadun, 2009, p. 174). *"Unorthodox approaches for conservation of biodiversity are needed"* (Lev-Yadun, 2009, p. 174). Humans *"should take [their] fate into [their] hands and conduct large (state or ecosystemwide) experiments with the introduction into other habitats of many species that are at risk of losing their natural habitats, a Noah's Ark approach[,]...but first in several highly damaged ecosystems"* (Lev-Yadun, 2009, p. 174). *"Waiting and doing nothing will certainly result in losing so many species that their loss might be much more harmful than the potential risks of the introductions....[At] this time"* serious *"measures must be taken, before it is too late"* (Lev-Yadun, 2009, p. 174). Noah's ark symbolizes salvation.

Chapter 5

Heaven

Christians' religious conceptions about fishermen may bifurcate from their comprehension of the actual occupation and the realities of fishing and trawling. Christians seldom associate present-day commercial fishing and trawling with paradise, and yet heaven is described by Jesus in Matthew 13:47 as being like a fisherman's net or a dragnet (Baarda, 1991).

> *'Once again, the kingdom of heaven is like a net that was let down into the lake and caught all kinds of fish. When it was full, the fishermen pulled it up on the shore. Then they sat down and collected the good fish in baskets, but threw the bad away. This is how it will be at the end of the age. The angels will come and separate the wicked from the righteous and throw them into the blazing furnace, where there will be weeping and gnashing of teeth. 'Have you understood all these things?' Jesus asked. 'Yes,' they replied. He said to them, 'Therefore every teacher of the law who has become a disciple in the kingdom of heaven is like the owner of a house who brings out of his storeroom new treasures as well as old''* (Matthew 13: 47-52).

Letting down a net may have referred to several similar forms of fishing. The first form, dragnet fishing, is known to date to the third millennium B.C.E. (Burge, 1998). Egyptians used a net with cork on the top and weights on the bottom, like a wall pulled along the coast. A boat could lead the net to sea and return it to shore; and then, workers sorted and distributed fish. In a second form depicted by ancient Egyptians, a circular net with a diameter of approximately 15 to 20 feet was cast by a single fisherman. Lead weighted the casting net, which landed on and captured fish. Fishermen entered the water to gather individual fish by hand or used boats to lift full nets. A trammel net, which continues to be used by contemporary fishermen, is a third kind of net fishing. Three layers were connected to a head rope and cork at the top and lead weights at the foot rope (Burge, 1998; Nun, 1999). The inner net was designed to flow loosely between the exterior nets. Using a method innovated by aquatic mammals and other fish, fishermen would scare schools towards a trap where their lives would end (Burge, 1998; Cusack, 2015). Fish vigorously would flee from harm into the net and become entangled in the loose inner net.

The kind of fishing described in Matthew is not specifically identified, but a parallel narrative about the judicious process described in Matthew is portrayed in Gospel of Thomas (Gospel of Thomas 8; Matthew 13: 47-52). "*Man is like a wise fisherman who cast his net into the sea he drew it up from the sea, full of small fish. Among them he found a large, good fish, that wise fisherman. He cast all the small fish down into the sea. He chose the large fish without difficulty"* (Gospel of Thomas 8). A plain reading demonstrates that the verses may reflect Semitic culture, and irrespective of their possible independence, they are connected by nuanced portrayals of fishermen. Contemporary popular analyses focus on apocalyptic interpretations of multitudes and selected fish contrasting with discarded fish—possibly meaning bad faith actors, unclean animals, or unchosen souls; yet, this focus seems to misrepresent and gloss over difficulties associated with commercial fishing because it takes for granted the parable's simplistic depictions of fishermen easily casting nets, catching abundant fish, and nonchalantly, albeit shrewdly, eliminating undesirable catch (Baarda, 1991; Clark & Wasserman, 1980; Ewherido, 2006; Wells, 2000). "*Matthew includes additional references in parabolic settings, making pronounced use of the apocalyptic image of 'fire'"* (Green, McKnight, & Marshall, 1992, p. 311). *"The angels gather the 'weeds' at the 'end of the age' and burn them with fire"* (Green, McKnight, & Marshall, 1992, p. 311; Matthew 13:40, 42). *"The same fate befalls the 'bad fish' in Matthew 13:50 and the accursed 'on the left' at the great judgment of the nations in Matthew 25:41-46"* (Green, McKnight, & Marshall, 1992, p. 311). "*Finally Matthew repeatedly describes the lot of the wicked with the emotive phrase 'weeping and gnashing of teeth.' Except for one parallel," "Matthew alone includes the phrase five times"* (Green, McKnight, & Marshall, 1992, p. 311). For ancient fishermen, *"[h]auling the net ashore, disentangling the fish, sorting them, and repairing the many breaks during the day took a lot of work,"* which is why the *"Old Testament uses the image of these 'entangling nets' to describe the futility of humanity"* (Burge, 1998; Ecclesiastes 9:12; Job 19:6-8). Fish and nets becoming entangled is part of fishermen's work, but each form of entanglement results in particular forms of grief and labor.

Modern-day fishermen describe the routine of casting a net and drawing fish as arduous (1 Peter 5:7; McKay & McKay, 2013; Psalms 55:22). "*You've been picking fish for a while"* (McKay & McKay, 2013). *"[Y]ou're about to pull the rest of the net in by hand, letting it spill onto the deck, fish and all"* (McKay & McKay, 2013). There is no faster technique; and rapidity is valuable. "*You and the other deckhands won't stop until the last of it is on board. You take a firm grip on either the cork line or the lead line"* (McKay & McKay, 2013). Both feet must be planted. *"[P]ut your hood up, and keep your face pointed at the deck as much as possible--a jellyfish in the eye isn't a lot of fun. Then the roundhaul starts. Fish come whipping over the stern roller at head-height, but you focus on putting one hand over the other"* (McKay & McKay, 2013). *"The net and the fish are knee-deep, and you take a step back to make room"* (McKay & McKay, 2013). "*Everybody's gasping for breath and forcing leaden arms to keep hauling. At last, the buoy on the end comes over the roller"* (McKay & McKay, 2013). Fishermen feel relief because there is a pause in action. "*You would collapse, but you're up to your waist in fish, so there's nowhere to flop. Your face burns in a sharp, stabbing way; the jellyfish really had it in for you this time. Your head is covered in blood, scales, and sea salt"* (McKay & McKay, 2013). The pain is negligible in comparison to the reward, $500. *"Right now you've got two hours to pick all the fish out of the tangled pile of net and get it ready to set again, and you're going to need every minute. You and the other deckhands stretch, crack stiff joints and bad jokes, and get to work"* (McKay & McKay, 2013).

The ease painted in the parables *"implies that at least in the view of this... [parable] there was no reason to think that the fisherman needed others to draw in the trawl net,"* which may have required a team of several men (Baarda, 1991, p. 378). *"Gospel of Matthew's identification of the kingdom of heaven as both a physical place and a normative concept"* may minimize, ignore, or reformulate widespread perceptions about severe conditions allegedly associated with commercial fishing, and *"[t]he conclusion to this is that ideas can be particularized...leaving the imagination to complete its formation"* (Roark, 2007, pp. 371-372). The parable allows Christians to envision an alternate reality that transforms fishermen's public identity and mythologizes the process of commercial fishing by making it seem validated by God, effortless, and preeminent (Wassell & Llewelyn, 2014).

"Fishing is often called the first industry," and traditionally fishermen have devised fishing methods and protocols that promote conservation (e.g. invasive species management) (Cato & Sweat, 2000; Jawad, 2006). In some cases, conservation propaganda may be a technique for generating public interest in fishing, noninvasive aquatic life, and utilization of local waterways. For example, evidence demonstrates that local authorities have offered thousands of dollars in rewards for bagged invasive species, but in some waterways, very few invasive species were caught, which may suggest that rewards were symbolic (Winkel, 2015). Christians' promotion of conservation

may align with Christian concepts of stewardship identified throughout the Bible (e.g. the story of Adam and Eve); but, conservation principles may not be supported by a plain reading of this parable about nets. Unlike present-day fishermen, who may capitalize on bycatch and freeze excess to conserve resources, economize, and maximize profits, heaven wastes bycatch because the fish are unfit and undesirable. Ancient fishermen and workers in the fishing industry froze, pickled, and salted fish to preserve as much as possible (Duncan & Derrett, 1980). In Matthew's parable, good fish are thrown into a basket, but bad fish are discarded (Matthew 13: 47-52). If the fish are rubbish, then the kingdom of heaven may cause all fish to meet their demise, similarly to fishermen, who catch native and invasive species, for separate reasons; however, this interpretation of the parable seems to be unconcerned with conservation.

Another possible interpretation is that bad fish pulled ashore were released into the water. This interpretation may suggest conservation, but it could imply that invasive species were released possibly indicating a lack of stewardship and conservation. Though the scripture is often interpreted to mean that the righteous will be gathered by angels while the wicked will be thrown into the furnace, the verse literally says that the righteous will be thrown into the furnace, which may be symbolized by the basket.

King James Bible adds robustness to the analysis. "*Which, when it was full, they drew to shore, and sat down, and gathered the good into vessels, but cast the bad away. So shall it be at the end of the world: the angels shall come forth, and sever the wicked from among the just, And shall cast them into the furnace of fire: there shall be wailing and gnashing of teeth"* (Matthew 13:48-50). Here, the parable ambiguously refers to the furnace after referring to the just. Bad fish are cast away, which may describe catch-and-release or suggest that bad or small fish were recycled as bait meaning they were cast on lines. *"Net fishing was the stock-in-trade," "and the Gospels,"* for example Matthew 17:24-27, *"point to Jesus' knowledge of this. Hook-and-line fishing was known but used far less since it yielded fewer fish, but Jesus once told his followers to catch a fish using a single line"* (Burge, 1998). Several scholarly interpretations of the parable suggest conservationism. "*The kingdom of heaven is similar to a dragnet (or seine)" "thrown into the sea and gathered creatures of every species; when it was full they dragged it onto the shore, and sat down and (sorting them) gathered the good (part of the catch) into containers, and threw out the rotten"* (Duncan & Derrett, 1980 p. 129). In this interpretation, every good part is kept, and only rotten parts are discarded. If some fish carcasses were rotten before they were netted, then perhaps conservation is reflected here because every effort was made to salvage the good parts; but, if the fish rotted after being caught, then wastefulness may be evident, which would fail to resonate with popular strategies for preserving fish used by ancient and contemporary fishermen (e.g. freezing).

Various versions of this parable use the term *"wailing and gnashing of teeth"* (Matthew 13:50). *"Wailing"* seems to be a pun on "whaling" (e.g. *"a large, good fish"* mentioned in the Gospel of Thomas 8), possibly alluding to Jonah; however, *"[t]he allusions to Jonah here cannot be followed up"* (Duncan & Derrett, 1980, p. 130; Lobsters Scream, 2007; Matthew 13:50). *"Gnashing of teeth"* may connote mastication, and along with the pun about whaling, suggest that future fishing and fish-eating would change and be augmented (Gospel of Thomas 8; Matthew 13:50). The parable may imply that Christian disciples would not be forbidden from eating non-kosher animals without scales, such as whales.

Gospel of Thomas 8 may reflect ancient Semitic practices of discarding or releasing unclean animals, even if the parable does not allude to conservation; yet, small fish are released and only one large fish is bagged, which perhaps implies or promotes conservation. Christians generally operate under similar principles. In the United States, each jurisdiction may impose on recreational fishermen certain bag limits and lengths for particular species in order to make fishing sustainable. For example, in Texas white bass must be at least ten inches, and the daily bag limit is 25; but, in Florida the bag limit is one bass at least 14 inches long (Florida Fish and Wildlife Conservation Commission, 2015; Texas Parks and Wildlife, 2015). Good judgment is exercised by adherence to regulations because conservation metes out and increases opportunities for recreation and profit over longer periods of time. Thus, these regulations are consistent with Gospel of Thomas' description of wisdom.

The Gospel of Matthew describes heaven as a net, yet present-day Christians are unlikely to view local fishermen, net casting, or trawling as being heavenly in the same context depicted by John of Patmos, who described heaven as a city made of gold, emerald, and jasper, or as a bountiful catch (Matthew 13:48-50; Revelation 21:1-21). Though emeralds and gold may be more glamorous than fish, fish in ancient times were coveted. Fish were a staple food and symbols of status. For example, fresh water fish were consumed by wealthy people (Murphy-O'Connor, 1999). *"[S]tories [abound] of the mania of fish lovers, such as the eunuch from Lampascus who wasted his fortune on tuna...[and the] poetic voice of Juvenal's fourth satire notoriously boasts of a fish bought for the price of a field in the provinces or worth more than the slave fisherman who caught it"* (Sick, 2015, pp. 10-11). While wealthy, middle, and poor classes loved preserved and fresh fish, *"the quantity of fresh fish available did not meet the demand. This inevitably pushed up the price"* (Murphy-O'Connor, 1999, p. 24). During Jesus' lifetime,

Galilee was a populated and wealthy area where olives, wheat, and wine were exported (Green, McKnight, & Marshall, 1992). Between 200,000 and 300,000 people lived in Galilee. The Sea of Galilee was replete with fish and the town of Magdala was renowned for dried fish. Though people in every economic stratum were present in Galilee and enjoyed fish, there was a large economic divide between the wealthiest and poorest inhabitants. A burgeoning middle class was more numerous than the upper class, but most occupants were laborers and tenement farmers in the lower class. Galileans were known for being stubborn and fearless. The lower classes maintained religious reasons for denunciating the Roman ruling class. Their social temperament increasingly fueled rebellion and revolution, which escalated in 40 A.D. Fish consumption by lower classes implied that theft had occurred (Murphy-O'Connor, 1999).

Generally, ancient people may have been infatuated with fish. "*One simple gauge of the importance of fish in the ancient world is the space given to the topic in the oldest encyclopedia"* (Murphy-O'Connor, 1999, p. 24). *"[T]he Deipnosophistai (The Learned Banquet, or more wittily, The Gastronomers), compiled around 200 A.D. by Athenaeus of Naucratis in Egypt"* (Murphy-O'Connor, 1999, p. 24). The encyclopedia listed approximately 1,250 authors and over 1,000 play titles. Abundant references to fish are "*scattered throughout*" the encyclopedia (Murphy-O'Connor, 1999, p. 24). "*[B]ook seven is entirely devoted to fish"* (Murphy-O'Connor, 1999, p. 24). The book is "*125 pages in the Loeb Classical Library edition. The contrast with meat could not be more striking: The Deipnosophistai has many references to meat, but the largest block of material is only two and a half pages long. These simple statistics betray an intense interest in fish"* (Murphy-O'Connor, 1999, p. 24). *"The importance of fish is further highlighted by the references in the gospels to people who eat fish and carry fish with them. That some of these references appear as metaphors or in non-historical stories does not diminish their importance as believable scenarios in a Galilean context"* (Hanson, 1997).

Any Christians believing in parables' plausibility may be tempted to view commercial fishing as easier, thus more heavenly, than it really is. Although rumors currently abound that commercial fishing can result in fast money, realities tend to vary depending on season, position, experience, catch, and other factors, and several media outlets, including popular television shows, depict extreme risks in commercial fishing, which tend to overshadow perceptions of profitability in a typical risk-benefit analysis undertaken by Christians. Ancient Christians also analyzed risk of fishing versus profitability (Murphy-O'Connor, 1999). *"Business and profit" "did not completely satisfy them"* (Murphy-O'Connor, 1999, p. 48). *"They looked for something more spiritual and were prepared to make sacrifices to attain it. Their background and training, however, ensured that they would carefully balance risk against gain. They were not gullible, and nothing in their personalities even hints at a tendency towards self-deception"* (Murphy-O'Connor, 1999, p. 48). Present-day estimates for average earning salary are somewhat unclear and unstandardized; for example, the range from $20,000 in six weeks as reported by a deckhand, who is the vessel captain's son; to $33,430 annual salary reported as an average figure by the Bureau of Labor Statistics for fishermen and fishing workers in 2012; to $200,000 for captains; between $3,000 and $10,000 per season for deckhands; and $20,000 per year for fishermen working two consecutive seasons as reported by *Houston Chronicle* (John, n.d.; Lindzon, 2015; McKay & McKay, 2013; U.S. Department of Labor, 2014). Some crewmembers may earn a day rate between $200 and $250 or a percentage of a vessel's gross or net income based on weight and sale price (Lindzon, 2015). A substantial share may result in fishermen earning tens of thousands of dollars weekly or monthly; yet, they could earn no income if catch weight or prices are very low. Some crewmembers could become indebted to captains depending on whether they required gear to begin working. Even if these figures seem heavenly compared to less desirable positions paying minimum wage, commercial fishing is allegedly risky and dangerous. "*[C]ommercial fishing the deadliest job in America relative to pay"* (Stevely, 2011). "*The average annual salary for U. S. fishermen is $27,880"* (Stevely, 2011). *"There are 116 deaths annually per 100,000 fishermen. Compare that with firefighters, who are paid a salary of $47,730 and have three deaths per 100,000. The second deadliest job relative to salary: loggers with $34,510 in pay and 92 annual deaths"* (Stevely, 2011).

Ancient fishermen may have had similar pay structure options that caused them to have an interest in the catch or only to have an occupational interest in making, caring for, and letting down nets (Duncan & Derrett, 1980; Hanson, 1997). There is some scholarly debate about ancient fishermen's economic status. The debate incorporates the story of Jesus asking several fishermen to drop their nets and follow him, possibly implying abandonment of worldly possessions and occupations (Matthew 4:19). Ancient fishermen *"could hardly be classed as 'entrepreneurs' in such a highly regulated, taxed, and hierarchical political-economy"* (Hanson, 1997). *"While thc boat owners/fishers may or may not have also been involved in fish processing,"* their occupations *"would not have made them wealthy, and certainly not 'middle class,' as many authors have contended, since the whole conceptualization of a middle-class is anachronistic relative to Roman Palestine. The 'surplus' went to the brokers and the ruling elite"* (Hanson, 1997). Fishermen surrounding Jesus may have had lower economic status making it somewhat easier to cast their focus from their occupations onto discipleship.

Christian society tends to behave as if cleanliness is next to godliness evidenced by their use the term *"clean"* to indicate both physical sanitation and moral righteousness and blamelessness (Corgan, 1996). For example, Jesus may have used a word like *"clean"* to mean *"kosher," "sanitary,"* or *"pure,"* such as in John 13:10-11: *"Jesus answered, 'Those who have had a bath need only to wash their feet; their whole body is clean. And you are clean, though not every one of you.' For He knew the one who was betraying Him; for this reason He said, 'Not all of you are clean.'"* In this context, if cleanliness is heavenly, then fishing is not heavenly because fishermen work in unhygienic and odorous environments. One fisherman explained a typically unappealing day aboard a fishing vessel. "*You live in a cabin the size of most people's bathroom with three other guys for two months"* (McKay & McKay, 2013). "*[Y]ou're in a regulation-length 32-foot-long boat"* (McKay & McKay, 2013). "*[You] commando-crawl out of your bunk, put on the same sweats you've been marinating in for at least five days, [and] slap on another coat of deodorant because you haven't showered in a week"* (McKay & McKay, 2013). You chow "*down some food, collect a few bruises and invent some new curses from pinballing around in the cabin"* (McKay & McKay, 2013). You must *"stomp into your Xtratuf boots, jam your heavy-rubber gloves on, clip on your life jacket, and stagger out on deck where you put on cold [and] clammy...heavy-duty rain gear* (McKay & McKay, 2013). Part of your job is "*[t]esting the limits of the human olfactory system"* (McKay & McKay, 2013). Unlike the parables, which segregate worthy from unworthy, all crewmembers may be sullied and pungent; however, consistent with the parable in Matthew 13:52 describing the good and just as houses filled with treasures, *"blood, scales, and...fish"* covering fishermen hoisting nets are actually valuable commodities and the odors that they cause represent treasure reaped by fishermen (McKay & McKay, 2013). Fishermen are like disciples bringing from the seas old and new treasure.

Chapter 6

Symbolic speech

A fish has symbolized grace throughout history and the contemporary era. Fishing is a ubiquitous symbol of Christianity; for example, Jesus repeatedly is depicted closely with fish, fishing nets, the Fish Gate, and aquatic environments. Catholic Popes have worn a Piscatory ring depicting a fisherman casting a net. Jesus' grace is evident in the ring because he loved Peter, the first Pope, who may be depicted on the Piscatory ring; and because he predicted that his death would glorify him immediately after the miraculous catch (John 21:1-14). Jesus addresses "*this adulterous and sinful generation*" in Mark 8:38. He is not specifying a demographic, but is addressing "*the people of Israel as a whole who have rejected him*" (Green, McKnight, & Marshall, 1992, p. 759). Simon Peter confesses to Jesus in Luke 5:8 that he is a sinner after Jesus performs the miraculous catch (Green, McKnight, & Marshall, 1992, p. 759). *"His confession comes in the presence of one whom he calls 'Lord,' indicating, at least, that Peter recognizes his own humility"* (Green, McKnight, & Marshall, 1992, p. 759). The ring demonstrates humility, not Jesus' resurrection, although that meaning may be derived from the symbol of the fish being hoisted from the sea.

Some symbols are uncertain while others have clearly been traced to particular stories or events. For example, Ichthys, meaning *"Jesus Christ Son of God Savior"* is not as certain in its history as the Piscatory ring. One reason may be that the fish symbolizes secret origins of Christianity. Another reason is its association with fertility among early Christians, despite their belief that Jesus did not have physical children, only spiritual offspring (Lawrence, 1991). Two aspects have been pivotal for modern westerners to grasp ancient meanings. First, *"the fish as 'support.'"* (Von Sadovszky, 1995, p. 253). Second, *"the fish as the symbol of fertility must have played an important role in ancient times and found its way as ΙΧΘΥΣ, (Ichthys) 'fish'* ⟜ *the favorite symbol of early Christianity interpreted as Iēsous Christos THeou HYious Sōtēr 'Jesus Christ Son of God, Savior'"* (Von Sadovszky, 1995, p. 253). *"This aspect of the semantic associations surrounding the fish was already treated by several scholars"* before it became faddish in the late 1900s (Von Sadovszky, 1995, p. 253). "*The visual similarity between a human calf muscle and a pregnant fish belly"* cognitively may have inspired associations with fish eggs (e.g. roe) etymologically memorialized by ancient speakers (Von Sadovszky,

1995, p. 253). *"[I]nvestigation of the semantic associations connected with the calf of the leg, fish roe, egg, small offspring, womb, belly would have led"* to complicated correlations with reproduction (Von Sadovszky, 1995, p. 253). *"The periodic return of the spawning season, the extremely large number of the fish-spawns, the importance of fish as food supply make fish a favorite focus of other associations. It is connected with good luck and fertility"* (Von Sadovszky, 1995, p. 253). *"The initials of the Greek word ΙΧΘΥΣ, ichthys, composed of the initials of the Greek words for Jesus Christ the Son of God, the [Savior],"* signify that a fish "*was a symbolical term"* (Goodhugh & Taylor, 1943, p. 919). It was "*in conventional use chiefly during the periods of persecution. Hence, and with allusion to the water of baptism, the early Christians sometimes called themselves Pisciculi, or fishes"* (Goodhugh & Taylor, 1943, p. 919). Undoubtedly, Jesus was the Son of God, but the meaning of Jesus being a "Son" may have been in question. To be a son meant to have an heir, but Jesus had no heirs and was not God's heir.

The Piscatory ring includes several symbols that express ideas beyond the miraculous catch, resurrection, and salvation. Ironically, it juxtaposes Jesus' suggestion that the disciples should abandon their nets and become fishers of men. "*The enormous value of the nets and the fishing boats to their owners or hirers requires no emphasis. To abandon one's fishing work would not be so curious, for one could return to it, since fishing is strangely irregular and casual (fishermen are not regular workers, nor good savers)"* (Derrett, 1977, p. 116). "*[T]o abandon one's nets is an odd thing to do. How characteristic of Jesus and his notion of recruiting! Adequate disciples must drop all competing interests"* (Derrett, 1977, p. 116). The Piscatory ring asks Christians and the Pope to *"remain for a moment longer at the material level"* (Derrett, 1977, p. 116). *"Yet to draw the fish from the dark depths which symbolized Sheol [i.e. Hades], and to bring them as a tribute to their Owner was a phase of the divine harvest. Jesus often spoke of the harvest"* (Derrett, 1977, p. 116). *"The flying dolphins represented in catacombs,"* for example *"[symbolize] emergence from mortal life! The various occupations from which the Twelve (not to speak of others) seem to have been called [emphasizes] that there was little or no restriction"* (Derrett, 1977, p. 116). Thus, it becomes a matter of availability, not profession. It seems that the disciples *"had the special powers of intuition, patience, cooperation, selfreliance, adaptability, flexibility and fitness to be on duty at night[,] which only fishermen possess"* (Derrett, 1977, p. 116). "*The fisherman...will go out to fish with little warning, and in ever high hopes, despite the innumerable chance features which impede success. From the point of view of the mission-field the conditions of fishing are not at all inappropriate"* (Derrett, 1977, p. 116). Many kinds of fishes will swim in the water. The *"fish are living souls healed by that water"* (Derrett, 1977, p. 117). *"The life given by that healing is immortality in spite of the presence of the fishermen!"* (Derrett, 1977, p. 117). The End of Days, known as the apocalypse, *"will see the end of death for those souls" "when they are reached by that water proceeding from the Temple"* (Derrett, 1977, p. 117). *"The process begins in Galilee, as well it might, since the present flow of the Jordan is the pattern which the prophet adopts"* (Derrett, 1977, p. 117). Waterflow in itself is an immortal phenomenon.

Contemporary Christians continue to celebrate and focus on symbols of immortality evident in circular patterns. For example, the press circulated a story about three fishermen, who celebrated a divorce, by placing a wedding band on the bill of a sailfish in Fort Lauderdale, Florida. Years later they angled in Miami and caught the same sailfish, who still wore the ring. The man symbolically had become betrothed to the fish and returned for the fish, like Christ will return for his bride. The focus of the story was not human-animal relationships, but rather, it was grace (*The St. Augustine Record*, 2007). The fish obeyed God literally and symbolically to complete the cycle.

Jesus likely drew from his immediate surroundings, cultural environment, and personal experience to metaphorize his mission and make his message appealing and distributable. His use of symbolism was designed to signify to disciples and crowds that they should choose to follow and they would receive his grace. Thomas Hobbes explains how Jesus layered his charismatic invitations using symbolic speech. "*Speech…is to [transfer] our [mental] [d]iscourse…into [v]erbal; or the [train] of our [t]houghts, into a [train] of [w]ords"* (Hobbes, 2013, p. 11). *"[T]hat for two commodities; whereof one is…[c]onsequences….[and] [a]nother is when many use the same words" "to [signify] (by their [connection] and order,) one to another, what they conceive, or think of each matter; and also what they desire, [fear], or have any other passion for, and for this use they are called [signs]"* (Hobbes, 2013, pp. 11-12). Jesus may have asked the disciples to throw down their nets so that he could control the symbolism of nets. *"Scandalous, because they be stumbling blocks,…make men to fall in the way of [r]eligion: as [i]njustice, [c]ruelty, [profanity], [a]varice, and [l]uxury. For who can believe, that he that doth ordinarily such actions, as…other men withall, for lesser faults"* (Hobbes, 2013, p. 104)*?* However, if Jesus controlled when the nets were used, then he could prioritize his mission over them when necessary, and control how they were used at other times. *"[Special] uses of [s]peech are these; [f]irst, to [r]egister, what by cogitation, [we] find to be the cause of [anything]"* (Hobbes, 2013, pp. 11-12). *"[T]o sh[o]w to others that knowledge which we have attained; which is, to [counsel], and [teach] one another"* (Hobbes, 2013, pp. 11-12). *"[T]o make known to others our wills, and purposes, that we may have the [mutual] help of one another"* (Hobbes, 2013, p. 11-12). *"[P]resent or past; and what we find things present or past may produce, or effect: which in* *[sum]"* (Hobbes, 2013, pp. 11-12). *"[T]o please and delight [ourselves], and others, by playing with our words, for pleasure or ornament, innocently"* (Hobbes, 2013, pp. 11-12). This symbolism defines Jesus' relationship with his followers and their relationships with fishing, a symbol of Christ and souls.

Chapter 7

Fish gate

Contemporary attitudes in Christian societies regarding commodification of fish and commercial fishing seem to reflect attitudes portrayed in the Bible; they also suggest historical continuity between practices in ancient Jerusalem and the present-day. However, Christian societies' policies and perspectives may demonstrate bias against non-Christian commercial fishermen despite the worth of their trade routes and exports (Cusack & Waranius, 2015). Furthermore, contemporary Christians' beliefs about the benefit of fish consumption may influence their choice to buy it.

In several scriptures throughout the Old Testament, the Bible refers to a Fish Gate in Jerusalem (Nehemiah 3:3). Generally, gates in Jerusalem were hubs, for example, a Sheep Gate may have been where lambs were traded; and at the Fish Gate, fish may have been commodified (John 3:10-16; Nehemiah 12:39). The Fish Gate may have been aptly named because the main commodity traded at this gate was fish; yet the Fish Gate was also a protective barrier, a transitory point for exiting and entering the city, and a portal for gaining access to the coast (2 Chronicles 33:14; Noonan, 2011). During Solomon's reign and during Ezra's era, Phoenicians used similar trade routes for timber (2 Chronicles 2:15; Ezra 3:7; Noonan, 2011). Abundant evidence (e.g. fish remains) produced over hundreds of years, such as during Middle Bronze II, Iron I and II, and Hellenistic periods, demonstrates that fish was a dietary staple in ancient Palestine (Murphy-O'Connor, 1999; Noonan, 2011). A market in the eighth century B.C.E. may have been responsible for importing into Jerusalem thousands of fish remains (Noonan, 2011). Approximately, 90% had been fished from the Mediterranean Sea (Noonan, 2011). While Egyptian species of fish were imported into Jerusalem, Egyptians did not control the market, although they were especially participatory during 11th century B.C.E. Between Iron Age II and the Achaemenid period, Phoenicians may have established in Jerusalem successful fish trade operations, such as shops located near the northern wall of Jerusalem at the northwest corner of the Temple Mount in Jerusalem, which involved sale of numerous kinds of fish and products, as well as wares decorated with fish, Phoenician-style ships, fishermen, and boats (Nehemiah 13:16; Noonan, 2011; Zephaniah 1:10-11). Mediterranean fish and fish products (e.g. paste) may have been sold at and near the Fish Gate on the Sabbath, along with jars of honey, pine nuts, oil, grain, olives, and wine. Trade possibly occurred during Neo-Assyrian and Roman periods; and while archeological evidence points to trade between the ninth and sixth century B.C.E., research suggests that trade and agricultural exportation continued after these eras.

Nehemiah, who was a cup bearer to the king, described regulating the Fish Gate in Nehemiah 12:39 and 13:16-19.

> *People from Tyre who lived in Jerusalem were bringing in fish and all kinds of merchandise and selling them in Jerusalem on the Sabbath to the people of Judah. I rebuked the nobles of Judah and said to them, 'What is this wicked thing you are doing--desecrating the Sabbath day? Didn't your ancestors do the same things, so that our God brought all this calamity on us and on this city? Now you are stirring up more wrath against Israel by desecrating the Sabbath.' When evening shadows fell on the gates of Jerusalem before the Sabbath, I ordered the doors to be shut and not opened until the Sabbath was over. I stationed some of my own men at the gates so that no load could be brought in on the Sabbath day* (Nehemiah 13:16-19).

The scriptures describe commodification of fish without reference to ethical treatment of animals or conservation. However, commerce is constrained by cultural and religious values. Harms committed in violation of the Sabbath result in regulation, which may impose conservation (Luke 6:9; Mark 3:4). Similarly, today in Christian societies, violations of trade agreements and regulatory schemes at ports, piers, and docks may result in civil and criminal interventions, remedies, and sanctions effectuated by the United States (U.S.) Coast Guard; federal and state governments; municipalities; North American Free Trade Agreement (NAFTA); U.S. Customs and Border Patrol; U.S. Drug Enforcement Agency; U.S. Immigration and Customs Enforcement (ICE); U.S. Department of Homeland Security; U.S. Department of Fish and Wildlife; U.S. Navy; and other American, foreign, or international organizations.

The U.S. is one of the largest importers of fish and fish products; yet, many Americans publicly are critical of some Asian fishermen particularly for their allegedly wasteful or damaging fishing practices. Christians use laws and regulatory schemes to enforce conservation practices on Asian fishermen and fishing enterprises throughout the world. For example, Christians, who rely on scientific findings, media reports, tourism, and other sources of information, tend to oppose shark finning (Clarke, 2008; Martin, 2007). Shark finning, fin possession, or sale of shark fins is illegal under U.S. federal law and in several states; and it publicly has been evaluated by Americans as wasting resources because some fishermen remove living sharks' fins and discard into the ocean their bleeding bodies (16 U.S.C. § 1857, 2010; Cal. Fish & Game Code §§ 2021, 2021.5, 2014; HRS § 188-40.7, 2015; NY Stat. § 13-0338, 2014; O.R.S. § 498.257, 2015; O.R.S. § 509.160, 2015; RCWA 77.15.770, 2014; V.T.C.A. Parks & Wildlife Code §§ 66.216-8, 66.2161, 2014). Some Asian American cultural advocates have claimed that these laws discriminate against Asian cultures in which shark fin soup is a delicacy (*The Huffington Post*, 2012). Yet, Christians' biases against shark fin soup may be justified by international awareness of shark finning, fisheries customs, and related ecological problems. Shark finning reduces populations of various shark species, some of whom are highly recognizable (e.g. Great Whites), causing them to be listed as protected species and further drawing public scrutiny, which seems to justify allegedly discriminatory impacts (Yick Wo v. Hopkins, 1886). Despite verbose opposition to certain wasteful commercial fishing practices, Christians may selectively, selfishly, and conveniently regulate fishing industries (Mittelbach, 2014). Furthermore, when they allegedly respond conscientiously to environmental concerns, they may seem to be biased in favor of countries with Christian heritage. For example, trawlers drag nets to catch copious species, but also net bycatch, such as sea turtles, jellyfish, porpoises, crustaceans, seabirds, and other species of fish. Bycatch may comprise the majority of a catch or several times the amount of the target species, with some estimates claiming that millions or billions of animals annually are unintentionally killed; yet, a sizeable percentage may be released. In 1998, the World Trade Organization (WTO) heard a case about requirements placed by the U.S. government on shrimp trawlers, which adversely affected Asian countries (WTO, 1998). In 1997, India, Pakistan, Malaysia, and Thailand complained to WTO about a U.S. importation requirement that banned certain shrimp and shrimp products. Under the Endangered Species Act of 1973, the U.S. had prohibited commercial fishermen from taking five different species of endangered or threatened sea turtles. U.S. shrimp trawlers in areas known to be sea turtle habitats were required to use nets with "turtle excluder devices" (TEDs). Public Law 101–102 § 609 (1989) banned importation of shrimp harvested using any means known adversely to affect protected sea turtles. Nations could certify implementation of regulatory programs that reduced incidental taking to rates acceptable to the U.S., which were also comparable with rates required for U.S. fishermen; or certify that their fishing locations did not threaten adversely to affect threatened turtles. This effectively required fishing industries throughout the world to institutionalize mechanical and technologic processes in conformity with U.S. standards. Countries that exported shrimp to the U.S. essentially were required constantly to use TEDs. Though WTO rules stipulate that nations have a right to protect the environment using trade actions, WTO held that nations' actions may not be discriminatory against WTO members. The U.S.'s requirements allowed Western hemisphere countries (i.e. Caribbean nations) extended transitional, financial, and technical facility and assistance. Thus, a lax regulatory scheme for Caribbean nations may have discriminated against Asian nations. Christians may argue that *"there is no international agreement that ensures the welfare and protection of animals."* or *"any international standard that regulates and defines the acceptable treatment of animals. [It is] [t]his lack of international consensus [that] leads to the current disparate treatment of animals around the world,"* not Christians' cultural preferences or biases (Favre, 2012). Furthermore, studies show that Christians' interest in conservation may relate to fear of resource scarcity more than treatment of animals or biases in some cases. For example, the value of catching, keeping, and eating fish may vary as fishermen associate fishing with conservation (Oh & Ditton, 2008). A study of 608 recreational fishermen from the U.S. found that their respect for and valuation of natural resources is directly related to dependence on those resources. Arguably, some bycatch could be processed and exported more inexpensively by Latin American than Asian companies; thus, American conservation schemes may originally have been developed to maximize resources while maintaining Christians' interest in protecting marine life (Cusack, 2012; Oh & Ditton, 2008).

Similarly to importation of culture through the Fish Gate into Jerusalem, commodification of fish by present-day Christians may be promoted by Christians' interest in Asian cultures and physiology. Non-Christians are the primary exporters of fish to Christians; yet Asians (i.e. Japanese) also lead the world in fish importation along with Americans (Bogomolova, Kozlova, & Kukharev, 2014; Bumble Bee, n.d.). In 2009, China, Indonesia, India, and Vietnam had most intensely developed aquaculture production and exportation, and they continue to refine and ramp-up production. China led the world in fish product exports, catching, and aquaculture production; Indonesia led in canned crustacean exports; and Thailand was one of the largest producers and exporters of canned tuna and crustacean products. Christians may accept a belief that eating some types of fish may be good for one's health; and this entices them to buy fish from Asia and Europe. Spain is a leader in canned tuna; and India has led the world in frozen and canned products, such as dried, smoked, and salted fish. Russia, Ukraine, and South Korea also produce and export notable amounts of fresh, chilled, and frozen products. Americans also buy fish from Latin America; for example,

Chile and Peru lead the world in fish meal and oil production and exportation. Americans may consume these products because they believe in health benefits, such as taking Omega-3 supplements to reduce heart disease. To promote benefits of eating fish, Christian societies often point to studies of non-Christian people, such as the Japanese, who primarily are Buddhist (Atkinson, 2011; Heine, 2016; Raji, 2014). Health trends associated with low meat and high fish diets include lower breast cancer rates, muscle strength in HIV-positive patients, fetal health, and lower neurological disease; however, Japanese society suffers from certain diseases, such as suicidality, more acutely than most Christian societies. Even though a study of 1,745 pregnant Japanese women found that higher intake of fish correlated with lower prevalence of depressive symptoms, fish consumption has not be found to relate to lower suicidality among Japanese men, a population with high suicide rates (Al-Ardhi & Al-Ani, 2008; Cotter, Mclean, & Craig, 2009; Miyake, et al., 2013; Poudel-Tandukar, et al., 2011). Nevertheless, Japanese and Asian commodification of fish has influenced Christians' health, culture, and economy. Christian commodification of fish is not only inspired by global economics and physiological benefits, but like the Phoenicians in Jerusalem, Asian aesthetics influence Christian importers.

Chapter 8

Bragging

Throughout the Bible, Jesus has been a savior; however, he has not been immune to Satan's ploys. *"A person with such a positive reputation will indubitably be envied, since in a 'limited good' world, Jesus' growing fame will be interpreted by some as their loss. "[P]eople will envy him because of his success and good reputation and...attack him for his honorable standing in the public's eye"* (Agedorn & Neyrey, 1998). He is a vulnerable hero, who accepts his destiny, but must destroy his enemy in order to succeed. He prevails in the end by elucidating mere fact—that God the Father is his father and he is saved. *"A principle is at stake, namely, Jesus' investment in the dynamics of gaining and maintaining honor"* (Agedorn & Neyrey, 1998). This trial was particularly difficult because at that time, salvation did not exist. *"Jesus foreswore the pursuit of honor and thus precluded envy from his disciples,...Jesus critically engages the value of honor in his cultural world....Although...he does not explicitly act to avoid envy, the new values and behavior which he enjoins will perforce prevent it"* (Agedorn & Neyrey, 1998). Clergymen during his era may have hated Jesus because of his position of power and status; however, not his bragging (Habakkuk 2:4).

Carl Jung said, *"The parallel I have drawn here between Christ and the self is not to be taken as anything more than a psychological one, just as the parallel with the fish is a mythological one"* (Jung, 1991, p. 57). Biblical writers' descriptions of fish illustrates this point. Their knowledge of and possible proximity to valuable fish may have caused them to experience an inflated sense of self-worth, which is salient in their writing about fish (Ezekiel 26:5, 14; Ezekiel 29:4; Genesis 1:26-28; Isaiah 50:2; Job 12:8; Job 41:1, 7; Psalms 8). When they depict fish as being overblown monsters, they are merely elucidating their own self-worth. Conversely, when they depict fish as being small and powerless puny creatures, they may be describing their self-worth in light of their distance from fish. The Koran also follows a similar pattern as evidenced in Surah 16:2-14. These writers operated *"in terms of a cultural system of values,"* which reflected their relative and subjective perception of self-worth (Agedorn & Neyrey, 1998).

Authors may have believed that there was *"limited good"* in accurately depicting fish, so they added grandiosity or inferiority in order to increase readers' intrigue in the subject matter (Agedorn & Neyrey, 1998). They may have been attempting to achieve status by way of comparison rather than through direct heroism. There are numerous ways *"whereby enviers might reduce an admired person to pity: (1) ostracism, (2) gossip and slander, (3) feuding, (4) litigation, (5) the evil eye, and (6) homicide"* (Agedorn & Neyrey, 1998). Writers of the Bible provoked to envy fish may not have observed that fish attempted to *"moderat[e] [their] desires and behavior which manifest ambition and attract attention"* in order to assuage envy (Agedorn & Neyrey, 1998). *"[A]ccording to the ancient world, they were either selfish brats who needed disciplining or simply honorless people that others do not have to regard or defer to*" (Agedorn & Neyrey, 1998). This idea may be a sign that the author was self-absorbed (Agedorn & Neyrey, 1998).

"[T]he concept of self-image, self-esteem and self-love has become a hot topic and the subject of much discussion. One of the big debates going on today is the place of psychology in Christianity" (Keathley, 2004). Self-image may relate to coping. For example, one study found that compassionate goals were less likely than self-image goals to correlate with heavy-episodic drinking (Moeller & Crocker, 2009). Yet, Christians may believe that self-centered *"coping motives"* lack trust and rely on selfish notions (Moeller & Crocker, 2009, p. 334). Perhaps Christians, who dislike psychology, are *"living in a day in which [people] have become lovers of self and our society has become self-centered and satiated with self and self-hyphenated, self-fixated words like self-actualization, self-esteem, self-worth, and self-fulfillment"* (Keathley, 2004). Christian clients may be more willing to trust mental health advisers, who wear Christian badges, such as Ash Wednesday ashes or a cross pendant, even if their methodologies do not directly incorporate Christianity (McCullough, et al., 2016). Badges may suggest to clients with Christian personalities that they will have an outlet for self-actualization during treatment. *"Ethical challenges swirl around the professional psychologist,"* who takes a Christian point of view while treating clients (McMinn, et al., 2010, p. 392). *"Unfortunately, the effectiveness of [B]iblical counseling has not been researched, so ethical issues of efficacy, competency, and welfare of the consumer"* are unknown (McMinn, et al., 2010, p. 392). Christianized methodologies may obfuscate the significance of professional credentials. Practitioners may be unable to show clients how to separate psychology from Christianity, which could result in clients becoming confused or experiencing additional problems. *"Some spiritually oriented approaches may be dismissive of psychotherapy"* and *"church-based ministry approaches" are unlikely to mix psychological modalities with faith-based realities"* (McMinn, et al., 2010, p. 395). *"[N]arrow religious dogma or adherence to strictly defined behavioral standards"* may impede treatment in a clinical setting because a *"program will depend a great deal on the nature of the church that sponsors*

it" (McMinn, et al., 2010, p. 395). *"Integrationist"* psychologists *"strive to look through two lenses simultaneously"* (McMinn, et al., 2010, p. 394). Nevertheless, *"if the client prefers Christian counseling to the intervention that the professional psychologist offers,"* then the client *"needs to engage in"* a *"discernment process"* (McMinn, et al., 2010, p. 396).

A Biblical *"self-concept or thinking properly about [oneself] in the light of God's grace is important to spiritual maturity,"* however. Jesus did not have self-help, self-esteem, or psychology (Keathley, 2004). *"The subject of [one's] self-concept or self-image creates a kind of paradox"* (Keathley, 2004). *"How do [Christians] avoid the self-centered approach and focus of the world and at the same time have a [B]iblical concept of self, a proper viewpoint of [their] own value and purpose that sets [them] free to serve"* (Keathley, 2004)? Right-thinking *"sets [them] free from those thoughts and feelings that tie [them] in knots," "ruin [their] personalities, [and] create false agendas and motives that"* cause people to become *"incapacitated"* (Keathley, 2004). *"That [humans] think" "about [themselves] is important and is even commanded in Scripture"* (Keathley, 2004).

"Ironically, quite contrary to our society today," the apostle Paul *"may not warn against thinking too little of ourselves"* (1 Timothy 1:15; Corinthians 15:9-10; Ephesians 3:8; Keathley, 2004). *"Paul is calling for thinking and personal evaluation based...on the facts of God and His grace"* (Keathley, 2004). Perhaps his lessons in 1 Corinthians 15:9-10, Ephesians 3:8, and 1 Timothy 1:15 mean that Christians *"are to look at [themselves] through the lenses of Scripture,"* not psychology (Keathley, 2004). Out of a concept of God, Christians develop *"solid spiritual maturity"* and *"ability to lead others"* (Keathley, 2004). They change so that they can become servants. "*Without a [B]iblical concept of self, [they] end up playing spiritual king-of-the-mountain and engage in promoting personal agendas to build up...sagging ego[s]. [Christians] seek from position, power, and praise what [they] should get from resting in God's grace"* (Keathley, 2004).

Poor *"self-image"* may be detrimental to Christians' *"energy and powers of attention to relate to others because [they] are absorbed with our own inadequacies"* (Keathley, 2004). *"That is especially true" "in the presence of people who remind"* Christians of their *"shortcomings or whose judgment about"* themselves and a Christ-like self-concept they may *"value and want to influence"* (Keathley, 2004). Under these conditions, Christians *"are so self-conscious that [they] cannot give sufficient attention to others"* (Keathley, 2004). Psychologists may describe this phenomenon as painful shyness, which may develop because others have failed appropriately to regulate their expectations and to intimate empathy to the painfully shy person (APA, n.d.). Whether self-image is imposed by psychologists, ministers, or other influences, *"many people perceive themselves according to a portrait they developed early in life from the messages they received from their environment...These may be good or bad..., but it is...perception that forms the basis of how most people feel about themselves"* (Keathley, 2004).

Because *"feelings of self-esteem and self-confidence rest on being able to take pride in [one's] achievements, it's not only okay, but healthy, to brag about"* oneself (Whitbourne, 2012). Psychologists may overanalyze bragging, and therefore be unable to provide a simple understanding of it. For example, a psychologist may suggest that indirectly calling attention to amazing accomplishments or personal qualities by claiming that a superior took note creates an epistemic conundrum for recipients because comments may lack veracity. Yet, directly calling attention to an accomplishment, such as possessing, catching, eating, or knowing about fish may seem to lack modesty, and may not compare to others' accomplishments. However, the bragger may suffer from an epistemological conundrum, which he or she overcomes by inflating or deflating fish's characters and bodies. *"Oddly enough, for whatever reason, although it's not okay to claim to be great, it is okay to be self-deprecating by reporting" "flaws"* to a psychologist (Whitbourne, 2012). The purpose of a clinical setting does not encourage people to *"lay claim to being smart, but it's okay to admit to being stupid"* (Whitbourne, 2012). Basking in reflected glory by flattering a therapist's participation in positive self-image may circumnavigate this problem, but also constrict the bragger's level of participation in bragging lest a line be crossed into direct bragging. Disclaimers precipitating bragging may alleviate some immodesty, but risk exaggeration resulting in bragging losing thrust and impact.

Chapter 9

Repressed American sexuality

Studies in Classic American Literature by D. H. Lawrence (1917) recognizes that Americans were comprised of Italians, Spaniards, British, Egyptians, Muslims, Christians, Chinese, and other groups, which caused American expression to develop a uniquely American tone (Cusack & Telesco, 2012; Cusack & Waranius, 2015). Americans may have perceived themselves as being an English-speaking mono-culture; but outsiders, such as the British, could clearly identify significant cultural and social differences between Americans and the British. Variability in ethnic roots among American descendants of European peoples influenced Europeans reading American literature, for example D. H. Lawrence, whose works profoundly affected American culture and society. *Lady Chatterley's Lover*, as a book and a film, has been held to be obscene or been blocked from public distribution by numerous courts (Cusack, 2017; Grove Press v. Christenberry, 1960; Kingsley International Pictures v. Regents, 1959; Lawrence, 2005; People v. Dial Press, 1944). Though Lawrence's work eventually failed to meet contemporary obscenity standards, and was ruled to be non-obscene in several cases, courts may have correctly analyzed the issue of whether his work was obscene. Support for this may be evident in the fact that Lawrence saw his work as adult subject matter (Lawrence, 2005). Perhaps Americans quickly identified Lawrence's work as mature and sub-textual because of his British writing style, which elucidated the parent-child relationship between England and the United States. Furthermore, Lawrence viewed classic American literature as being sweetened or dulled, like children's stories, when it was written using a mature quality and for adult audiences. "*WE like to think of the old-fashioned American classics as children's books. Just childishness, on our part. The old American art-speech contains an alien quality, which belongs to the American continent and to nowhere else. [When] we insist on reading the books as children's tales, we miss all that*" (Lawrence, 1917). Lawrence suggested that one reason for British readers' preference for reading American literature as children's stories was that *"It is hard to hear a new voice, as hard as it is to listen to an unknown language. We just don't listen. There is a new voice in the old American classics. The world has declined to hear it, and has babbled about children's stories"* (Lawrence, 1917). He claimed that Americans also despise their own adult voice because it resounds the cacophony of carried experiences. Lawrence claimed that the human race does not fear innovative thoughts because humans can tidily classify and dismiss new ideas. However, actual experiences cannot be summarily dismissed. The world "*can only dodge. The world is a great dodger, and the Americans the greatest. Because they dodge their own very selves"* (Lawrence, 1917). *"It is the shifting over from the old psyche to something new, a displacement. And displacements hurt. This hurts"* (Lawrence, 1917).

Lawrence said that art-speech is a "*subterfuge*" for which people should be grateful because they have the willpower to unveil the device (Lawrence, 1917). Art-speech may provide experiences through emotional provocation; "*[a]nd then, if we have the courage of our own feelings, it becomes a mine of practical truth. We have had the feelings ad nauseam. But we've never dared dig the actual truth out of them, the truth that concerns us, whether it concerns our grandchildren or not"* (Lawrence, 1917). Lawrence views art-speech as a form of expression. His professional use of speech expresses sexuality.

Like many analysts, Lawrence correlates American expression with Puritanism and tense moralism. "*The artist usually sets out" "to point a moral and adorn a tale. The tale...points the other way, as a rule. Two blankly opposing morals, the artist's and the tale's. Never trust the artist. Trust the tale. The proper function of a critic is to save the tale from the artist who created it"* (Lawrence, 1917). Lawrence suggests that Americans' need to exhibit innocence and spiritual vacancy relates to an absent-minded desire to forget European history. He questions why European artists migrated and developed into American artists. He believes that American artists anticipated that the public expected them to lie, and they were willing to lie. Lawrence blamed audiences for expecting lies. Negating the assertion that European settlers and refugees sought religious freedom, Lawrence claims that England *circa* 1700 A.D. provided greater freedom of worship than the New World. Freedom in England was earned by Englishmen, who fought for it and remained in England. Travelers' motive was to escape, "*[i]n the long run, away from themselves. Away from everything. That's why most people have come to America, and still do come. To get away from everything they are and have been. 'Henceforth be masterless'* (Lawrence, 1917). Yet, this does not equate to true freedom. Lawrence views this as being "*the reverse"* of freedom (Lawrence, 1917). Constraints caused hopelessness because their identities were defined by what they rejected, not by what they affirmatively approved or desired (Lawrence, 1917). The American Dream is a fantasy promised to those, who attempt to become wealthy, because if they can prove their worth, then positively they will be affirmed (Weber, 2002).

Lawrence, whose work was attacked in American courts, fought the spirit of his critics, thereby further inciting them. He resents that Americans brag about freedom, but lynched him. The "*free mob*" caused him *"abject fear of his fellow countrymen,"* which he observed as being typical of all Americans (Lawrence, 1917). He feels that dissimilarity was one cause of the mob mentality. He may feel that the sexual tone in his work could have been expressed by an American; and yet, may not have been published had it been produced by Americans.

Lawrence identifies Christianity as the overlord, who scared the pilgrims from England. *"[T]here is a positive side to the movement. All that vast flood of human life that has flowed over the Atlantic in ships from Europe to America has not flowed over simply on a tide of revulsion from Europe and from the confinements of the European ways of life"* (Lawrence, 1917). Lawrence views "*revulsion"* as key to emigration (Lawrence, 1917). *"It seems as if at times man had a frenzy for getting away from any control of any sort. In Europe the old Christianity was the real master. The Church and the true aristocracy bore the responsibility"* (Lawrence, 1917). Their mastery of the people resulted in "*the great drift over the Atlantic"* (Lawrence, 1917). "*What were men drifting away from"* by "*breaking the bonds of authority"* (Lawrence, 1917). They were seeking absolutes.

Lawrence's ideology suggests that they were driven by their restrained sexuality. The Church, an external force, may have controlled their social interactions, to some extent, but their internal controls, such as morals, and their tolerance for the expression of unwelcomed morality in their private affairs converted the church from a societal leviathan into a monster haunting their lives and restricting their expression.

In his poem, *"Whales Weep Not!,"* Lawrence (1971) may transcend society and personify human sexuality by depicting whales' sexuality. Under the sea, in animal bodies, his characters can been queer, aroused, sexual, competitive, pagan, erotic, and tolerant. He may also believe that their location, in addition to their species, sets them apart from human Europeans and Americans. They were united in a place that they felt was their "*home"* (Lawrence, 1971). A "*great spirit"* has a *"vital effluence, different vibration, different chemical exhalation, [and] different polarity,"* and generates *"great reality"* (Lawrence, 1971). *"The Nile valley produced not only the corn, but the terrific religions of Egypt"* (Lawrence, 1971). *"The Chinese in San Francisco will in time cease to be Chinese, for America is a great melting pot"* (Lawrence, 1971). Each being is rendered from his environment and a "*great spirit,"* who brings forth manifestations of sex, love, abundance, and freedom (Lawrence, 1971).

Lawrence may express his sexual desires by imagining himself as a whale. His poem may be a meta-exploration for his desire to unearth his true sexual identity and freedom from sexual compulsion. Humans "*are not free when they are doing just what they like. The moment you can do just what you like, there is nothing you care about doing"* (Lawrence, 1917). "*Men are only free when they are doing what the deepest self likes"* (Lawrence, 1917). "*[G]etting down to the deepest self" "takes some diving" "[b]ecause the deepest self is way down"* (Lawrence, 1917).

Ultimately, he understands that Americans are driven by fear of starvation, poverty, and other motivators that drive the workforce. Suppression builds motivation to facilitate upward social mobility. Only the wealthy, who inherit money and opportunities, are free from stand-in parents. Yet, they are subject to their parents' wills and wants.

America is rife with hardship and tension. Liberty is garnered by willpower carved from "*THOU SHALT NOT"* (Lawrence, 1917). The first order of business is "*THOU SHALT NOT PRESUME TO BE A MASTER. Hence democracy"* (Lawrence, 1917). Tension results from sexual and economic oppression that they fled from, but propagate in America. "*Instead of focusing on self-restrained reproductive sexuality, they focused on financial prosperity. In each scenario they sublimated expression in order to stir disquietude and incite results. Therefore, they conscripted their own will to become productive"* (Lawrence, 1917). They avert confrontation with the self, but cannot dispel the part of each human that sexually and economically craves a master. Americans may deny their need to feel "*glad obedience to the master they believe in, or they live in a frictional opposition to the master they wish to undermine. In America this frictional opposition has been the vital factor. It has given the Yankee his kick"* (Lawrence, 1917). *"Only the continual influx of more servile Europeans has provided America with an obedient [labor] class"* (Lawrence, 1917). Their gratitude and submissiveness dissipate once they drop anchors (i.e. have children). Americans' "old man" remains in Europe, like a parental figure. *"Somewhere deep in every American heart lies a rebellion against the old parenthood of Europe"* (Lawrence, 1917). Try as they may, Americans always regret their lingering subordination by European dominance. Adolescent embers of unwillingness smolder incandescent thoughts of rebellion and impatient opposition. Corrosive tension drowns Americans' happiness along with their memories of European methods. They become unremittingly masterless. *"But one dare not say this of the Pilgrim Fathers, and the great old body of idealist Americans, the modern Americans tortured with thought"* (Lawrence, 1917). Americans torture themselves because they wish to be idealists, but are self-interested; they wish to be free, yet depend on boundaries that they want to break; they desire to be governed fairly, yet fled greater rights in search of freedom; and toil for wealth under an illusory ideology of constraint (Lawrence, 1917). He may describe them as being masterless and self-tortured because they were poised to replace their masters' control and become the parents.

Lawrence finds truth in a pattern of lies. As a reader and an observer of American culture, he understands that expressive literature, such as fictional works describing torrid romances, may arouse readers and permit them to experience sexual pleasure. Art-speech titillates Lawrence because *"it prevaricates so terribly"* (Lawrence, 1917). He simultaneously celebrates and condescends art-speech because it possesses the power to lie. He believes that people constantly lie to themselves, but their inconsistency consistently paints an interpretable pattern. That pattern is truthful. This is *"[l]ike Dostoevsky posing as a sort of Jesus, but most truthfully revealing himself all the while as a little horror"* (Lawrence, 1917). *" [Y]ou can please yourself, when you read The Scarlet Letter, whether you accept what that sugary, blue-eyed little darling of a Hawthorne has to say for himself, false as all darlings are, or whether you read the impeccable truth of his art-speech"* (Lawrence, 1917).

The sexual pleasure experienced by using speech may be similar to the experience of a religious narrative and indoctrination. However, it may only be possible to break-free momentarily, when the work is taken as an adult narrative. Only in putting away childish things can a reader express and possibly manifest his or her most personal directives (I Corinthians 13). He identifies a trend in American culture that is presently the subject of great angst (Ecclesiastes 9:12; James 1:13-14). Yet, he suggests that what contemporary Americans believe is a new threatening wave of intolerance and abjection is actually a fundamental feature of Americans' identities.

Chapter 10

Explanations

The question of why fishermen fish is central to understanding the psychological and social relevance of fishing to contemporary Americans. The apparent answer is hunger. However, fishermen are called to participate in a variety of human-animal interactions at sea, for example to rescue animals. This divergence from the plan to eat is reminiscent of Jesus and the miraculous catch (John 21:5-6). *"These are faith stories"* (Marrin, 2011, p. 22). Jesus went to the Sea of Galilee to call the disciples to him, but found them fishing. They were reluctant to respond to him, and therefore, saw him as an apparition. Though they knew that he had risen from the dead, they responded to him because he presented an opportunity to fish. They experienced the miraculous catch because Jesus ordered the fish to appear in the fishermen's net. However, in marine environments the etiology of miraculous catches or dangerous encounters is less clear.

This myth begins in John 21:5. In this tale, fishermen catch so many fish in their nets that they are practically unable to transport the fish. Numerous videos on social media depict *"flying fish"* jumping into boats (Weisheipl, n.d.). For example, flying carp, also known as silver carp, jump from the water if startled (*The Times of Northwest Indiana*, 2013). A depiction of a high powered speed boat on the Wabash River in Indiana illustrates that silver carp will jump into the air. Even at the rapid rate of a speed boat, a few carp may land in the boat when the river is plentiful; however, fishermen may be unwilling to assist fish into the water, and subsequently may eat the fish. Their initial intentions may not have been to harvest fish by using their boats. Fishermen may be reluctant to return marine life to the water because the animals are excessively heavy and large or because of their muscle movements. For example, a dolphin jumped onto a tour boat (Youtube.com, 2016). At first, the passengers were repulsed by the dolphin's movements and allowed the creature to struggle for life. Eventually a wet towel was placed onto the head of the dolphin, who was ushered into the water. The act symbolized mercy, compassion, and obedience to the law and international principles of fisheries conservation. Saint Thomas Aquinas says the Peter experiences a similar situation (Weisheipl, n.d.). "*Peter asks them to go fishing, saying, I am going fishing*" (Weisheipl, n.d.). Aquinas describes the spiritual component as a *"mystical interpretation"* signifying "*the work of preaching"* (Weisheipl, n.d.). *"I will make you fishers of men"* (Matthew 4:19). Peter's affirmative, self-directed activity bears a "*mystical"* significance to the followers and to the audience because "*he is taking the others to share in his concerns and preaching"* (Weisheipl, n.d.). Aquinas find this "*mystical"* message in Exodus 18:22*: "So it will be easier for you, and they will bear the burden with you"* (Weisheipl, n.d.).

When fishermen go fishing they expect to catch food. Although they may anticipate sport and participating in cycles of life and death, they may not be able to foresee that they will be called to participate in the cycle. For example, they may rescue marine animals from being preyed upon by other animals, who may or may not be within the fishermen's food web. *"Their actual fishing seems to go against Luke (9:62): 'No one who puts his hand to the plow and looks back is fit for the kingdom of God.' And it is clear that Peter had given up his work as fisherman"* (Weisheipl, n.d.).

In some situations, fishermen are asked to save marine animals. A video taken on a boat depicts a seal apparently escaping a pod of killer whales (Fraser, 2016). The seal wiggles onto the stern slipping past the motor. The passengers ridicule his plight, but do not force him to abandon the boat. He is helpless as the whales are circling, but he is also well taken care of by the passengers, who do not force him off. In the end, they cheer for the seal, who survived what likely would have been mistreatment by whales, who wanted to use him as a toy, eat him, or end his life. The passengers may not harvest and eat the seal because that would be against the law in many geographical areas and against customary and contemporary culture throughout the world.

Fishermen may become injured when they attempt to fish. Saint Thomas Aquinas' analysis of Saint Augustine's analysis of the miraculous catch draws connections between injuries and fishing (Parker, 1842). *"Why then did he return to it and look back? I answer, with Augustine, that if he had returned to this work of fishing before Christ's resurrection and before seeing Christ's wounds, we would think that he was acting out of despair"* (Parker, 1842; Weisheipl, n.d.). Numerous videos depict marlins injuring fishermen, such as one video that graphically shows a marlin piercing a fisherman's mouth (Youtube.com, 2007). The man was injured, but survived. *"But now, even after Christ returned from the grave, after they had seen his wounds, and had received the Holy Spirit by Christ's breathing on them, they became what they were before, fishers of fish [not of men]"* (Weisheipl, n.d.). Marine animals, for example whales, destroy fishing vessels (Euro News, 2010). *"We can learn from this that a preacher can use his abilities to earn the necessaries of life and still preserve the integrity of his apostolate, if he has no other means of sustenance"* (Weisheipl, n.d.). This indicates that Saint Thomas Aquinas may have believed that with other available means of sustenance, preachers should not fish. One may extrapolate that perhaps Aquinas believed that exploited animas ought not to be harvested unless necessary for survival. Perhaps a more accurate application to the whale-fishing vessel scenario may be that he believed that a whale would be justified in crashing a fishing vessel if the whale believed that doing so would rescue fish or result in the whale consuming human flesh.

Whales may destroy more vessels than are reported. For example, the disappearance of a small boat at sea may not be unusual (Squires, 2016). Whales may bump, crash, and destabilize boats. Whales and other marine mammals do not often crash boats and eat humans because they are not a part of whales' food chain. In fact, some marine mammals, including whales and dolphins, have helped humans to survive at sea (Dreadfin Records & Clips, 2013). For example, they have led surfers, drowning sailors, and boaters to shore, intervened to prevent attacks, and acted as buoys. *"For if St. Paul learned an art he did not previously have in order to obtain the food he needed, so as to avoid being a burden to others, Peter could all the more do this by using his own skill"* (Weisheipl, n.d.).

Humans may benefit from marine mammals fishing. For example, killer whales in Australia cooperated with humans when they led baleen whales into Twofold Bay for slaughter (Toft, 2009). "*For thousands of years, killer whales have hunted the great baleen whales in every ocean on earth, yet only in one place have they ever co-operated with humans to hunt whales, and then largely only with one family, the Davidsons"* (McKee, n.d.). *Killers of Eden* is an astonishing tale about an implied *"contract between man and one of nature's most powerful and intelligent creatures"* (McKee, n.d.).

Killer whales returned annually to Eden from the Antarctic. For over a century they hunted mating baleen whales. The Davidson family symbiotically worked with generations of killer whales. *"A few members of the pod of orcas would swim right into the mouth of the [K]iah [R]iver where the Davidsons had their two isolated houses on the opposite side of the bay"* (McKee, n.d.). They would indicate the performance of their work by slapping or breaching the surface, called *"flop-tailing"* by the Davidsons, who would row to the killer whales' location (McKee, n.d.). The whales' bioluminescent trails visible during new moons also communicated their positions. Killer whales killed the baleen whales for their tongues and lips. The whalers harvested the baleens' carcasses; and in exchange, would share the tongues and lips of baleen whales, who they had caught, with the killer whales. The remainder of killer whales' kills were not immediately available to whalers. Carcasses would float to the surface after two days. Then the Davidsons would boil their carcasses to produce oil (i.e. *"trying out"*) (McKee, n.d.). Their reciprocity was termed *"law of the tongue"* by the Davidsons in the spirit of conservation and sharing (McKee, n.d.). They symbiotically rescued each other from harm (e.g. sharks, ropes, and lines). Symbiosis is when *"The others agree to this,"* and the offeror says *"We will go with you"* (Weisheipl, n.d.). The family abstained from motorboats, and only relied on rowboats. *"Sometimes motor launches were offered for use as pick-up boats in case of accidents or to tow whales to shore"* (McKee, n.d.). Whaling was declining by the 1920s. The Davidsons' neighbor, *"J. R. Logan would occasionally give the row boats a tow out to a chase with his yacht the 'White Heather', but no bomb-gun or harpoon was ever fired from a motor boat in [T]wofold [B]ay"* (McKee, n.d.). *"The Davidsons avoided using explosive 'bomb-guns' to catch whales because the concussive noise greatly distressed the killers,"* and breached their implied contract (McKee, n.d.). Contemporary technological tools allegedly clashed with and defeated traditional "*cultural whaling*" (McKee, n.d.).

In 1900, whalers worked with more than one dozen killer whales, including Old Tom, Hookey, Humpy, Jackson, Cooper, Charlie, Typee, Stranger, Kinscher, Montague, Old Ben, Young Ben, Sharkey, Jimmy, Jimmy Albert, Brierley, Youngster, Walker, Skinner, Big Jack, and Little Jack. Photographs and facts about individual whales demonstrate whalers close association with the pod and their desire to preserve their memories. For example, Old Tom was the most prominent male; and Typee was murdered at a beach. After he was murdered, the pod disappeared. Many permanently left, but only one half-dozen returned the following season. Immediately the killer pack left the bay for the remainder of the season and the following season only six returned. Although *"it has been suggested that" "disappearance of the killers was a result of dwindling food supply, large scale hunting of eastern coast humpback populations did not actually occur until the 1950s,"* one "*half century after Typee's killing and the Eden pack splitting in two"* (McKee, n.d.). The Davidsons realized that during World War I, *"the killers were being deliberately shot and killed by Norwegian whalers working from Queensland who were oblivious to their non-competitive assistance to the Eden whalers"* (McKee, n.d.). "*Old Tom himself passed away in 1930, 30 years after Typee," "yet still 20 years before large scale whaling for humpbacks in Australia"* (McKee, n.d.). Old Tom's skeleton is preserved in the *"Eden Killer Whale Museum and bears testament to the extraordinary tales told about him"* (McKee, n.d.). Similarly, churches are museums to Christ's memory. They testify about why he was a fisher of souls. *"They went out and got into the boat; but that night they caught nothing"* (Weisheipl, n.d.). Christians may explain their past actions and challenges as resulting from spiritual battles with spiritual entities, forces, Christians, and unsaved individuals. These understandings may influence why they fish.

"Many scholars find two separate traditions (as appearance and a meal story) in the account of the miraculous catch of fish (21:1-14). Others...have argued for a unified tradition. In either case," there appears to be a *"combined tradition and redaction into a theological whole"* (Green, McKnight, & Marshall, 1992, p. 686). *"The primary thrust is the power of the Risen One which is made available to the church"* (Green, McKnight, & Marshall, 1992, p. 686). The purpose is symbolically, but not literally, described, which *"has led most scholars to apply this to the church in mission, both in terms of evangelism" "and fellowship"* (Green, McKnight, & Marshall, 1992, p. 686). *"Jesus' appearance by the Sea of Galilee is often linked with a similar miracle at the call of the disciples in Luke 5:1-11"* (Green, McKnight, & Marshall, 1992, p. 686). Thematic cogency is evident because Jesus requests radicalized subservience and then grants *"an astounding catch of fish to demonstrate the new call to 'catch' people"* (Green, McKnight, & Marshall, 1992, p. 686).

The primary theological component of the narrative involves disciples. They fished for an entire night, but caught no fish. Then, on the shore, they beheld a stranger. Their subservience to Jesus apparently may be doubted because they failed to recognize their master. Their Risen Lord is identified after he performs a miracle and fills their boat with fish. Their attention is caught along with the fish they take into their vessel. A secondary component is the assured and promoted success of their mission. Christians following Jesus were warned of adversity, but promised followers on Earth supernatural authority over evil, and a peace in heaven. *"This theme is premised on the great size of the catch—153 large fish"* (Green, McKnight, & Marshall, 1992, p. 686). Several scholars interpret the size of the catch to boast of Christians' success.

Fishing was physical and mundane. Disciples were persuaded to leave their work, which had been unprofitable on the occasion of the miraculous catch prior to the *force majeure.* Yet, Matthew, a successful tax collector, also left his position, which required mental effort. *"One absorbs the mind, and hinders" "spiritual concerns"* (Weisheipl, n.d.). *"There is another kind of work which can be done without sin and without absorbing the mind, such as fishing and things like that"* (Weisheipl, n.d.) Therefore, in spite of his failure, Peter did not sin when he professionally fished. Mundanity did not equate with profanation. This is one reason why Peter was chosen as Pope, so that he could serve all types of souls.

Animals and humans go into the sea together to fish, which is why Peter was such a good symbol of the kingdom of God. His dual identity mirrors Christ. At birth he was named Simon, meaning *"reed"* (Marrin, 2011, p. 22). His name Peter, meaning *"rock,"* was *"given to him by Jesus in the famous scene at Caesarea Philippi, where perhaps the most problematic pun in all of history was uttered by Jesus to describe Peter's role as the 'rock' on which the church would be built"* (Marrin, 2011, p. 22). The combination moniker, Simon Peter, "*best describes the paradoxical figure who continued to exhibit both strength and weakness throughout his life as recorded in the New Testament"* (Marrin, 2011, p. 22). Peter's papacy is representative of why people fish.

Chapter 11

Solomon

King Solomon's renowned knowledge is a basis for law in several contemporary cultures and ancient civilizations (Goodhugh & Taylor, 1943). I Kings 4:29-34 says, *"God gave Solomon wisdom and [it]....surpassed the wisdom of all the sons....For he was wiser than all men....He also spoke 3,000 proverbs, and his songs were 1,005. He spoke of trees,...he spoke also of animals and birds and creeping things and fish."* Builders and engineers from surrounding nations helped Solomon build his temple and empire. Hebrew affluence and dominance reached an apex during Solomon's reign. Legends recited by theology, history, and archeology scholars lend support to Biblical archives that recorded Solomon's affluence, prosperous expansion, "*the splendor of his court, and the vast extent of his intellectual acquirements. His subjects did not appreciate his plans; commerce, which flourished so much during his reign, was quite abandoned after his death; and the Jews retrograded to their old agricultural and pastoral habits"* (Goodhugh & Taylor, 1943, p. 1245).

Solomon was *"no doubt acquainted with many species"* (Easton, 2005, p. 260). "*There was a regular fish-market in Jerusalem,*" *"as there was a fish-gate which probably was contiguous to it"* (Easton, 2005, p. 260). *"Half a mile westward, in the filthiest part of the city, the Pescheria (fish-market), may be seen four Corinthian columns and three pilasters of white marble, and part of an ancient pediment, nearly hidden by surrounding brick walls"* (Bartlett, 1879, pp. 24-25). *"Some of the first man-made pools ever built were constructed by Solomon, who had pools of water filled with fish built outside of the Temple"* (Stacy, 2010). Solomon's knowledge of fish may have been exceptional (Goodhugh & Taylor, 1943). Solomon was a distinguished scholar. He produced seven treatises on the subject of natural history; however, these documents have not survived. His ideas are some of the most popular in the world. He authored Proverbs, Ecclesiastes, and Song of Solomon (i.e. Canticles and Song of Psalms) (Goodhugh & Taylor, 1943). Contemporary values reflect his knowledge of relationships between fish and the general ecosystem. Rationales may be scientific, but their bases are ancient. *"[A]ncient reservoirs near Bethlehem, which once supplied water for it and Jerusalem, do not date back to Solomon...This area is a fitting place to reflect on the love poetry of Scripture known as the Song of Solomon or Song of Songs"* (Kirk, 1992, p. 205).

Israelites used *"fish pond (piscine) for fresh-water fish that could be caught and served to bathers"* (Magness, 2012, p. 182). These are dissimilar from *"Solomon's pools"* referring *"to Herodian water collection systems south of Bethlehem"* (Magness, 2012, p. 372). Tomb paintings provide ample evidence that other societies acknowledged the magnificence of Egyptians' fish ponds, which regularly were constructed in villas. *"[T]he master of the house occasionally amused himself in fishing. The Jews, it seems, likewise constructed similar ponds* (Goodhugh & Taylor, 1943, p. 1063). In Song of Solomon 7:4, Solomon romances his bride, saying *"Thine eyes are like the fish-pools in Heshbon."* Descriptions of Solomon's fish pools may have *"general acceptance, though without any solid evidence"* (Magness, 2012, p. 177). However, it is contemporary beliefs about ancient methods that serve as foundations for and justifications of contemporary practices.

Some pools were decorative, but others were profound trenches, for example Bethesda. A pool may be a *"small pool of rain-water in a deep gully"* (Robinson, 1838, p. 265). Other pools were *"excavated in the soft limestone rock on which the city is built"* (Robinson & Smith, 2015, p. 324). Some measured *"360 English feet in length, 130 feet in [width]..., and 75 feet in depth,"* and may be used as a *"reservoir"* layered with stones and plaster (Robinson, 1838, p. 434). *"The main dependence of Jerusalem for water at the present day is on its cisterns"* (Robinson & Smith, 2015, p. 324). Enormous cisterns *"anciently existing within the area of the temple" "supplied" "by rain water"* and by *"aqueduct[s]"* were centerpieces of Israeli life (Robinson & Smith, 2015, p. 324). *"[A]lmost every private house in Jerusalem"* had *"at least one or more cistern[]"* (Robinson & Smith, 2015, p. 324). Fish pools or *"simply 'pools'"* were reservoirs stocked with fish (Easton, 2005, p. 260). *"John 5:2 is to be translated, 'There is in Jerusalem by the Sheep Pool the site with five porticoes called in Hebrew"* (i.e. Aramaic), *"'Bethesda'"* (Green, McKnight, & Marshall, p. 41). North from the Temple square, a location may be found for a pool, *"whose name has been passed along"* in a diverse and assorted array of forms, such as *"House of Fish"* (*"i.e., baptismal symbol"*) (Green, McKnight, & Marshall, p. 41). The pool steadily has been documented by records from ancient Christian pilgrims and contemporary digs (Green, McKnight, & Marshall, p. 41). *"These pools were primarily designed to supply Jerusalem with water"* (Easton, 2005, p. 557). *"From the lower pool an aqueduct has been traced"* (Easton, 2005, p. 557). *"Solomon's Pool"* may *"attest to the existence" "of an earlier pool"* (Mare, 1987, p. 177). *"Solomon was anointed at" "the Pool of Silam. Thus the name Solomon's Pool would have been particularly appropriate"* because *"this pool is located in the right place between Pool of*

Siloam and Ophel" (Mare, 1987, p. 177). *"This mound serves to carry the aqueduct from Solomon's pools into the area of the mosk"* (Robinson & Smith, 2015, p. 267). It carries *"the water through Bethlehem and across the valley of Gihon, and along the west slope of the Tyropoeon valley,"* which "*finds its way into the great cisterns"* (Easton, 2005, p. 557). The pools and their attendant fluidity represent solid and pliable aspects of Solomon's kingdom and present-day Christians.

"Fish abound in the Mediterranean" and likely did when Solomon built the Temple Mount in 960 B.C.E. (Easton, 2005, p. 260). Therefore, reservoirs may have been indulgent, status symbols, or culturally relevant. Some reservoirs *"serve[d] in the collection of rain water"* (Mare, 1987, p. 168). They also terminated aqueduct systems. They were pleasure pools; some were bathhouses; they served as watering spots for sheep and other animals; some were used for irrigation; and others were fish pools, etc. (Easton, 2005; Mare, 1987). The Israelites adeptly implemented irrigation. Cultivation of seeds, pomegranates, figs, and vines demonstrates Israelites' proficiency. Their use of irrigation is also evident in their unhampered fish consumption (Goodhugh & Taylor, 1943, p. 1054; Robinson & Smith, 2015). Some pool waters were disturbed, perhaps they were whirled. *"Steps allowed to descend in the pool but how the waters came to be disturbed is as yet uncertain"* (Green, Brown, & Perrin, 2013, p. 53; Isaiah 7:3; Isaiah 22:9-11; 2 Samuel 2:13; 2 Samuel 4:12). The New Testament and other ancient sources illustrate that *"[m]ost of the population consisted of lower-class Jews who lived in simple but sturdy houses in farms and small villages, and supported themselves through...fishing"* (Magness, 2012, p. 201). Solomon may have had pools like other ancient rulers in that region where the *"centerpiece of the promontory palace"* was a robust fish-stocked pool (Green, Brown, & Perrin, 2013, p. 176). *"Rows of columns surrounded the pool on all four sides, creating a peristyle porch with the open-air pool in the center. The pool was on the lower part of the promontory, with another part of the palace located on a higher terrace to the east"* (Green, Brown, & Perrin, 2013, p. 176). At that time, Solomon's kingdom represented globalization and continues to inspire Christians to embody and assimilate other cultures into Christendom. Various states within America may share culture and resources in a spirit of collaboration, conservation, and Christianity.

Las Vegas, Nevada is a desert city using reservoirs to avoid water scarcity. Las Vegas uses water from the federal Hoover Damn, a *"world-renowned structure"* (U.S. Department of the Interior, 2015). *"Hoover Dam is a testimony to a country's ability to construct monolithic projects in the midst of adverse conditions"* (U.S. Department of the Interior, 2015). It is located in Black Canyon between Arizona and Nevada. Las Vegas is approximately 30 miles northwest of the dam. The Colorado River flowed without interruption through the diversion tunnels for almost two years. *"As winter low water approached,"* the "*Colorado River began to back up behind Hoover Dam to form Lake Mead. For the first time in history, the Colorado River was under man's control"* (U.S. Department of the Interior, 2015). Control exhibited humans' attunement with nature and the elements.

Human demand and evaporation affect water levels. The city is growing too fast for its water supply (Tanner, 2007). Without sufficient water supplies, Las Vegas could cease to attract tourists. Disappearance of the tourist industry would impair the local economy. For more than a decade, Las Vegas has actively prevented this.

Water conservation is the key management strategy for Las Vegas water supplies.

Conservation strategies could target new hotels and casinos to include a water conservation plan and pay increased taxes for the study of and implementation of new water management resources (Tanner, 2007). They may also encourage the expansion of tourism, even though it increases water needs, because as long as the city can pay for water, then it will not run out of water (Tanner, 2007). Strict enforcement of conservation or austerity measures may include heavy fines for violators. *"Cash for Grass"* has had the most success (Shine, 2015). This program pays homeowners $1.50 per square foot of water-efficient desert landscaping replacing grass in a yard. Approximately 50,000 homes and 5,000 businesses have replaced 172 million square feet of grass to save 9.6 billion gallons of water in 2015, which is approximately ten percent Southeastern Nevada's allocation from the Colorado River. Two hundred million dollars have been spent to replace grass, but this is counterbalanced with deterrent programs, such as those that prohibit development of new homes, businesses, and apartments with grassy front yards and restrict backyards from being more than 50% grass. Unfortunately, conservative resource expenditure may not equate with sustainability. Las Vegas could experience a water-shortage before 2100.

Southern Nevada Water Association (SNWA) collaborates with Colorado River Basin states to delay shortages by storing water supplies in Lake Mead (SNWA, n.d.). Lake Mead is a reservoir for Nevada formed by the Hoover Dam. *"The high-water line is at 1,229 feet above sea level. At this elevation, the water would be more than 7 1/2 feet over the top of the raised spillway gates, which are at elevation 1,221.4 feet. All lands below elevation 1,250 have been retained for reservoir operations purposes"* (U.S. Department of the Interior, 2015). The reservoir covers approximately 248 square miles and extends upstream nearly 110 miles toward the Grand Canyon and 35 miles up the Virginia River. At its widest point it spans eight miles; and through the canyons it is approximately a few hundred feet in width. It may hold approximately nine trillion gallons and store two years of flow from the Colorado River. Annually it attracts nine million swimmers, boaters, skiers, anglers, and nature lovers. Lake Mead National Recreation Area is managed by the National Park Service. It was the first federal recreation area and is one of the most popular tourist destinations in the United States. This is significant because Nevada's water supply at the Hoover Dam and Lake Mead is managed by the federal government and the Hoover Dam straddles two states. The relationship may be analogized to King Solomon's kingdom, which was divided between North and South Israel. North Israel received the bulk of the resources. Though the Colorado River has been in a drought for several decades, it continues to be recognized as a source of electricity at a rate of two cents per kilowatt-hour for Southern California, Nevada, Arizona, Los Angeles, and ten cities downstream (Kuckro, 2014). However, the drought continues to raise fears that Nevada will lose important water and power supplies. *"The West has suffered years of drought with the Colorado supplying less water to Lake Mead"* (Tanner, 2008). Lake Mead provides resources to Arizona, California, Nevada, and northern Mexico. *"The lake created by Hoover Dam provides 90 percent of Las Vegas' water and is less than half full, giving the edge of the lake a bath tub ring visible even far away by air"* (Tanner, 2008). Conservation strategies and efforts between 2002 and 2015 have helped reduce per capita use by 37% even though an additional 500,000 people resided in Nevada during that timeframe (Las Vegas Valley Water District, n.d.).

Researchers predict that Las Vegas' primary water source will be dry within a decade (Tanner, 2008). A study conducted at the Scripps Institution of Oceanography at the University of California San Diego predicted 50% probability that Lake Mead will vanish in less than ten years. SNWA data confirms these findings and shows that the current drought is worsening; however, economic downturn in the state has alleviated population growth and subsequent consumption and depletion (SNWA, n.d.). The water source from Lake Mead is insufficient. Inefficient pumps from Lake Mead will require more than $45 million in upgrades, but these upgrades cannot likely prevent the situation from worsening over time. The upgraded pumps, which would pump a second intake site at the lake, would improve drinking water pumping capacity by 200%. Unfortunately, the project will delay between three to five years—a timeline that Las Vegas residents and industries cannot afford. Though Nevada is attempting to store water in Arizona and Nevada water reserves, many believe that this reserve will not be sufficient. Also, it is clearly not an independently sustainable solution. The SNWA has stated conservation cannot be the only strategy. Wide-head turbines have been installed to maximize energy irrespective of water levels. The generators' new control systems increased the speed at which they may be brought online, ramped-up, and powered down. Plant efficiency and relative energy production is at an all-time high.

Chapter 12

Idolatry

Christianity may be at odds with fanatical and greedy corporate culture prevalent in Christian societies because some corporate culture and practices may be idolatrous. The foundation of Christianity is monotheism. *"If one believes God has partners in God's work or compartmentalizes God, this is idolatry"* (Jaffe, 2008). Like Christianity, Judaism and Islam are built on faith in one God, who is allegedly the same God in all three religions. In Judaism and Christianity the Ten Commandments first stipulate in Exodus 20:2 that there is only one God. The second commandment in Exodus 20:3 is that idolatry is prohibited. The second commandment *"is the negative complement to the first commandment and a renunciation of idolatry"* (Jaffe, 2008). Jews, Christians, and Muslims are not supposed to reject idolatry in support of atheism (Surah 3:67; Surah 87:14). *"Idolatry also does not [mean]...replacing the Jewish,"* Muslim, or Christian *"God with another Higher Power....Idolatry means denying God's oneness"* (Jaffe, 2008). Rather, the second commandment is a foundational principle of monotheism inherently requiring faith in, prioritization of, and submission to one God.

In his studies of totemism Emile Durkheim examined idolatry (Durkheim, 1995). Totem poles depicting animals representing ancestors are effigies empowering society's self-worship. His studies reflect Biblical warnings against totemic idols found in Deuteronomy 4:15-19.

> *You saw no form of any kind the day the Lord spoke to you at Horeb out of the fire. Therefore watch yourselves very carefully, so that you do not become corrupt and make for yourselves an idol,... whether formed like a man or a woman, or like any animal on earth or any bird that flies in the air, or like any creature that moves along the ground or any fish in the waters below. And when you look up to the sky and see the sun, the moon and the stars—all the heavenly array—do not be enticed into bowing down to them and worshiping things*

> *the Lord your God has apportioned to all the nations under heaven* (Deuteronomy 4:15-19).

The Bible acknowledges humans' capacity for self-worship, commemoration of past greatness, and desire to depict their sense of connection to the divine, but the scripture warns Israelites to abstain from self-worship or any form of idolatry. God refers to worship of natural and sentient beings (e.g. fish) as too common for Israelites, who God has appointed to be the chosen people. Thus, monotheism is like a monogamous spiritual relationship in which the chosen people only worship God.

The Christian Bible repeatedly warns against idolatry, depicting it as inferior and subordinate to monotheism. Christians are left with no doubt that the Bible opposes any force, nation, god, ritual, ruler, or thing that is exalted or relied on more than the one true God. For example, Christian and Jewish scriptures describe Dagon, a god worshiped by the Philistines (Johnson, 2011). Dagon has been described by non-Biblical sources as appearing to be a merman with the tail of a fish and the upper extremities and head of a man. In Chapters Five and Six of the Book of 1 Samuel, Dagon, worshipped by the Philistines, is defeated by Israel's God. After the Philistines stole the Ark of the Covenant, and brought it to Dagon's temple, Dagon's idol toppled. Dagon's hands and head broke off, literally and figuratively dehumanizing him leaving only a fish's tail intact. This event may suggest that all humans are subject, while animals are relatively immune, to the Ark's power or to God's covenant with the Israelites. Perhaps, this event suggests that fish are part of God's covenant with the Israelites. Within a few scriptures, the Bible explains that Dagon's priest and worshipers invented a ritual superstitiously to circumvent the area where the idol broke; thereby defining idolatrous rituals by their idol's weakness (Cusack, 2015). The Book of 1 Samuel also explains that the Philistines moved the Ark, *"[b]ut after they had moved it, the LORD's hand was against that city, throwing it into a great panic"* (1 Samuel 5:9). The scripture emphasizes the power of God's hand, which was broken on Dagon's statue. It may also insinuate the fact that fish do not have or need hands, which further highlights the Philistine's error in creating Dagon's idol. The Philistines decided to return the Ark to the Israelites because it had caused rat infestations and tumors. With the Ark, they sent an apologetic offering of two calves and several gold casts of rats and tumors. This again suggests animals' relative immunity to the Ark and the covenant. The Israelites sacrificed the cows to God and accepted the gold models. Hands are also contrasted against idolatry of Dagon the merman in the story of Samson (Judges 16:25). After Samson is captured, he is brought into Dagon's temple to be humiliated.

> *When they stood him among the pillars, Samson said to the servant who held his hand, 'Put me where I can feel the pillars that support the temple, so that I may lean against them.' ....Then Samson reached toward the two central pillars on which the temple stood. Bracing himself against them, his right hand on the one and his left hand on the other, Samson said, 'Let me die with the Philistines!' Then he pushed with all his might, and down came the temple on the rulers and all the people in it* (Judges 16:25-30).

Two hands represent idolatry in each story, but the Israelites' God only uses one hand to curse the Philistines. In Jewish lore, the priestly class blesses congregants by extending their arms toward the congregation, placing their thumbs together, and separating their middle fingers from their index fingers; thus, two hands become one hand, and ten fingers become five. In contemporary Christian societies, God's hand continues to be used to represent monotheism. Preference for right-handedness is consistent throughout the Old and New Testaments, including when Jesus instructs some disciples to cast their fishing net to the right side of their boat to fish (John 21:6). Dozens of political groups operating in Christian societies also depict a single hand to represent human forces (e.g. order). The power fist, for example used by the Jewish Defense League headquartered in the United States with chapters in several other Christian societies, represents unity and solidarity. However, the power fist is usually left-handed, not right-handed. Sometimes it is used to symbolize antiestablishment political agendas, which disrupt traditional principles used to govern Christian societies.

Christian monotheism is explained using the trinity: God the Father, Son, and Holy Spirit. Although Christians validate faith in the trinity by using scriptures in the New and Old Testaments, *"[s]ome Jews believe Christianity to be idolatry for this reason"* (Jaffe, 2008). Allah is supposed to be synonymous with Ha Shem, the verbalized name of God in Judaism. Some scholars believe that Christian and Muslim idolatry may have been foretold in Deuteronomy, which allegedly predicted people worshiping wood and stone (Deuteronomy 4:28, Deuteronomy 28:36, 64; Deuteronomy 29:17). Some scholars and theologians speculate that Deuteronomy alludes to Christians' *"worship"* of Jesus' cross and Muslims' *"worship"* of the Black Stone, which is part of the Kaaba in Mecca (Hawting, 1999).

A few scholars and religious pundits have argued that Islam is rooted in idolatry; yet, scholarly knowledge about pre-Islamic Arabian paganism is somewhat scant. Contemporary Orthodox Muslim views of idolatry may be more conservative in contrast to Orthodox Christian and Jewish views because Orthodox Muslims do not make or display any images of animals irrespective of whether images are worshiped. The influence of aniconism in unorthodox Muslim and nonreligious Arab communities is evident because it is the basis for heavy use of geometric patterns in art and textiles. Islamists go so far as to prohibit photography depicting sentient beings, whether living or dead (e.g. pictures from fishing trips). A corporation operating in or appealing to a highly politicized Arab region would be less likely to use a fish logo than a company appealing to Orthodox Christian or Jewish communities. Companies operating in politicized Muslim regions may use logos depicting trees, the moon, stars, or other non-sentient beings.

Several corporations operating in Christian societies depict fish to represent corporate culture, brands, and corporate persons. Some corporations managed, operated, or owned by Christians use fish logos, like the symbol used by the early Christian church, to identify Christian business practices or operators (e.g. Amadeus fishing vessel). Although some fail to incorporate Christian principles into their business practices and dealings, the symbol of the Christian fish creates corporate culture and branding aligning consumer awareness with Christianity, which may ingratiate the brand to Christians.

Among Christians, corporate logos are not generally considered to be idolatrous; but their popularity (e.g. Florida Marlins) may represent how the public idolizes certain products, some of which may be addictive, controlling, and the center of focus in a person's life (e.g. baseball fanatic or gambler). Like ancient religions that used statues of fish to embody and symbolize deities and deities' qualities, corporate logos depicting fish may identify corporations' power and grandiosity, or sometimes, corporate persons. Thus, a logo may depict a nebulous powerful person, who operates by enriching, destroying, and altering groups of individuals' lives; wherein the potency of the corporate person is determined by how much stock certain individuals (e.g. employees or consumers) put into their faith in the fictitious person's deeds, rights, and power.

Corporations, embodied by their logos, may be god-like. In Catholics' minds, public corporations, private corporations, and other organizations, "*exist as means to the end of human flourishing, without intrinsic value. To ascribe to a corporation the basic rights of a human being, therefore, is not just mistake, but a type of idolatry*" (Whitney, 2014). It places "*a fiction of our own making on an equal status with a human being whose end is ordered by God*" (Whitney, 2014). Idolatry surrenders to a "*fictional entity the authority to make moral decisions on behalf of natural persons*" (Whitney, 2014). Christian society, comprised of adherents commanded not to worship idols before God, has been accused of corporate idolatry by religious watchdogs, foreign cultures, the popular press, and proponents of family-life. Corporations have been accused of acting as gods, and employees have been accused of putting corporations before God; for example, by working on the Sabbath (e.g. Sunday), failing to tithe, and absorbing corporate culture to an extent that supersedes their public and personal identities as Christians. Christians allegedly have idolized revenue above morality by failing to hold corporate America responsible for greed, misrepresentations, and fraud. *"[S]hareholders themselves have....[idolized] short-term profits and share-price increases rather than engaging recalcitrant managers in discussions about corporate governance or executive pay"* (*The Economist,* 2010). These foibles have been partially responsible for economic downturns that perpetuated poverty.

Further demonstrating disconnects between Christian monotheism and idolatry of money and corporate fanaticism, some companies selling Christian products may openly break the law, thereby placing greed above the law and the commandment not to steal. Some Christian merchandise corporations slightly alter famous logos and brands to communicate Christian messages on t-shirts, hats, and other merchandise. For example, one t-shirt bearing the phrase *"A-bread-crumb and Fish"* borrows Abercrombie and Fitch's logo to promote the story of Jesus feeding the multitude by multiplying the loaves and fishes. Such merchandise expresses a form of brand fanaticism. By illegally appropriating corporate logos, fanatics declare their willingness to break copyright laws and the Ten Commandments in an attempt to syncretize Christianity with certain brands. Each year, retailers in America sell approximately $4.6 billion of Christian merchandise. "*[S]ome are spoofs or spinoffs of commercial logos or brand names. Many such goods are illegal"* (Reeves, 2009). Some companies may be "*unaware*" that *"their names are being copied or"* companies *"don't put up a fight for fear of being labeled anti-faith"* (Reeves, 2009). "*[L]egal parodies of commercial trademarks are protected under the First Amendment, but such religious products generally don't fall into that category"* (Reeves, 2009).

Courts have repeatedly discussed Fair Use, which would likely be Christians' defense for their infringements (Copyright Act of 1976). One case discussed whether *The Cat NOT in the Hat! A Parody by Dr. Juice*, a summary of the O.J. Simpson trial written in a rhyming style, constituted a parody under Fair Use (Copyright Act of 1976; Dr. Seuss Enters v. Penguin Books USA, 1997; Katz & Wrinn, 1996). *The Cat in the Hat* is a story about a cat, who intrudes into the lives of a fish, Carlos K. Krinklebein, and two children while their mother is not home (Dr. Seuss, 2005). The story follows a particular rhyming pattern. The Ninth Circuit held that the alleged parody did not meet the standard for

Fair Use because it was not transformative resulting in a new work or meaning (Dr. Seuss Enters v. Penguin Books USA, 1997). Even though it mimicked *Cat in the Hat,* it did so lazily, not as a parody of *Cat in the Hat* (Dr. Seuss, 2005; Dr. Seuss Enters v. Penguin Books USA, 1997). The alleged parody not only heavily relied on portions of *Cat in the Hat,* it completely followed it thematically and narratively (Dr. Seuss, 2005; Dr. Seuss Enters v. Penguin Books USA, 1997). The Fair Use defense does not seem to apply to Christians' infringement on corporate logos because their use is not intended to comment on corporations, parody corporations, or create a new message about corporations. Rather, their use lacks creativity and relies on public recognition of popular corporate logos to sell merchandise. Yet, Christians may stealthily and unethically rely on corporations' unwillingness to risk losing goodwill in highly publicized lawsuits against companies promoting Christian scriptures. Thus, while Christians' may avoid overt idolatry, their abuse of copyright law greedily, fanatically, and lazily negates Christian principles.

Muslims' avoidance of idolatrous logos may fulfill Islamic mandates; yet their obedience to Allah, in this aspect, may seem insignificant in comparison to some Muslims' serious disregard for animals resulting from some corporate practices. Muslims have been commanded to act as stewards and embrace animals as symbols of Allah's characteristics, mandates, and works. Allah is not physically symbolized by depictions; but, Allah is signified by living creatures and nature. For example, "*There is not an animal that lives on the earth, nor a being that flies on its wings, but forms part of communities like you....[T]hey all shall be gathered to their Lord in the end*" (Surah 6:38). Another example is, *"He who takes pity on a sparrow and spares his life, Allah will be merciful to him on the day of judgment"* (Surah 24:36). Despite these instructions, numerous examples of corporate damage to environmental resources and aquatic ecosystems are routinely reported in the Middle East. The Jordan River has been damaged by greedy, negligent, and uncaring business practices that fail meaningfully to incorporate Islamic values and demonstrate corporate idolatry. "*Sixty years ago, the lower reaches of the river in which Jesus was baptized carried 1.3 billion cubic meters of fresh water through its banks. It powered a hydroelectric plant"* (Hauser, 2007). Presently, the Jordan River's flow has been diminished to almost nothing with only an approximate ten percent of the original flow remaining. Of this residual current, around half flows from meager tributaries, subterranean spring water, and the Yarmouk River. The Yarmouk River "*begins in Syria and joins the Jordan six miles south of the Sea of Galilee. The other half of today's river is raw sewage, runoff from agriculture and fish farms, and saline water, diverted from springs north of the sea"* (Hauser, 2007).

Approximately half of the world's population, including Muslims and Christians, view the Jordan River as a holy place even though the river is terribly contaminated. Hebrew and Christian scriptures repeatedly reference the holiness of the river, which is supported by Islam's teaching that Jesus was a prophet born from the Virgin Mary (McLelland, 2009). In Deuteronomy 34:5, Moses stood on the river's edge before his death and looked out to the promise land. The book of Mark describes how the Jordan River was used to baptize Jews and early Christians. (Mark 1:9-10) The Holy Spirit descended on Jesus as a dove after he was baptized in the Jordan River. Even though a pristine portion of the river continues to be used for baptism, baptism in some parts of the river could lead to disease and contamination. *"[T]he demands of modern life in a water-starved region, decades of violent conflict and the kinds of abuse and neglect have conspired to bring the river to the brink of ecological death"* (Hauser, 2007). Contamination not only affects local people and religious pilgrims, it affects three continents with religiously and ecologically diverse populations. "*Running through the lowest spot on earth, the lower Jordan gathers at the ecological intersection of Asia, Africa and Europe"* (Hauser, 2007). Assorted animals, plants, insects, and other living creatures "*find their northern and southern limits in the valley, including the Palestinian Mountain Gazelle and the Yellow Flag Iris"* (Hauser, 2007). "*An estimated 500,000 birds migrate through the valley every year"* (Hauser, 2007). Some scholars and religious leaders have called Jews, Christians, and Muslims "foolish" for neglecting to care for the Jordan River because of religious conflict; yet, the major culprits are corporations, and consumers, who place profits and economic value above ecological ethics and applicable religious morals and mandates. In some senses, the filthy spots of the river are like idols to corporate greed and power. Compartmentalization of monotheism from corporate practices harming fish may be idolatrous (Jaffe, 2008).

Chapter 13

Nile river

The Israelite people were exiled from Egypt after God cursed the Egyptians by killing the firstborn sons of people living in Egypt (Exodus 7:18, 21; Halley, 2000; Isaiah 19:8; Numbers 11:4-5; Psalms 105:29). Before the final curse, God sent nine curses, including turning the Nile River to blood. This act most certainly killed all the fish, which were a valuable commodity at the time. The exile of the Israelites is written about in Psalms and Isaiah. Jews discuss this myth in Numbers.

Fish were abundant in the Nile River (Smith, 1861). They continue to be a staple. *"The Nile on this account was anciently worshipped, and the plague in which its waters were turned to blood, while injurious to the river and its fish"* likely swiftly impacted religious beliefs, but did not last long (Smith, 1861, p, 497). It may have occurred during an inundation failure that resulted in famine, thereby further shaking Egyptians' faith. All of the fish in the Nile likely died, but the water may have washed away all the blood within two months when the banks were inundated. Israelites' faith may have been tested because in exile they lacked fish. *"The river...abounds in fish, after which the Israelites longed in their journey through the desert,...as it was the main article of subsistence"* (Goodhugh & Taylor, 1943, p. 940). The Lake of Tiberias, for example *"is full of fish of various kinds"* and *"some of the same species of fish are met with here as in the Nile"* (Goodhugh & Taylor, 1943, p. 995). They may have been near fish, but the Bible does not provide evidence that they ate fish while in exile; rather, they suffered from hunger (Exodus 16:3; Numbers 11:5-6). However, they did not starve or dehydrate because God provided for them, unlike the Egyptians. *"The river Nile was turned into blood, and the fish died, and the river stank, so that the Egyptians loathed to drink of the river (Ex. 7:14-25)"* (Easton, 2005, p. 553). Without the Nile river, the Egyptians faced bleak conditions.

God may have caused the Israelites to suffer so that his miraculous assistance did not cause them to become arrogant, complacent, weak, or entitled. 2 Thessalonians 3:10 says *"If anyone is not willing to work, let him not eat."* God may have wanted the Israelites to experience and arrive at an explanation for why in this limited circumstance, they would neither work nor starve. They had eaten better food as slaves, but were liberated to dwell in agrarian societies and Jewish culture, which is undeniably connected to harvest, food, and feasting. Christians continue to encounter opportunities to witness oppression/restoration and curse/blessing dichotomies that elucidate God's mercy and desire for people to sustain themselves. Individuals, who feel oppressed, directly or empathetically, may acutely be aware of others' suffering (Tanner, 2016). For example, many avid fishermen have observed that suppression of tribal fishing rights continues to correlate with bigotry (*U.S. v. Washington,* 1975). Judge George Boldt decided that treaties between Indian nations and the United States signed in the mid-1800s had reserved to natives specific rights at their accustomed places to fish. Tribes established their right to participate in fisheries management with the government. Recreational fishing opportunities may vary between indigenous and nonindigenous Americans. Some Americans may interpret this to mean that Natives historically were oppressed people, who needed to be protected; whereas others may interpret this as a cultural distinction codified by the government, which breeds jealousy among fishermen. The difference is self-referential. It may depend on a host of factors, such as economic prosperity, confidence, and self-reliance, which contribute to or determine one's success. Situational and environmental factors may indicate how one should perceive rights particularly when enforcement compromises one's expression and liberty. Every moment has the ability to elucidate voluntary attitude shifts, which determine political perspectives, such as Jesus being the Son of God or a Christian savior. His outputted agenda was dependent on his attitude, surroundings, and particular mission.

Another example is that female survivors of abuse may learn to fish rather than relying on their abusive partners for food. The book *Teach a Woman to Fish: Overcoming Poverty Around the Globe* discusses stories of women, who learned to be self-determined and self-reliant (Sharma, 2014). However, some people may link violence against women with recreational violence (*The Brush Back,* 2003; U.S. v. Stevens, 2010). Some critics have suggested that fishing correlates with fish-related violence, which in turn may influence interpersonal and social paradigms that correlate with human victimization. Thus, incongruent attitudes toward fishing demonstrate a common link that may lead to separate outcomes, work paradigms, and policies. In at least one Mexican tale, a fish is depicted as being reliant on a king's orders, which is similar to the story of Jonah that serves as a synchronistic allegory about Jesus (Boatright, Hudson, & Maxwell, 1964).

Chapter 14

Food

Sacrifice is the meaning of food. Christ's sacrifice is symbolized by dishes intended to celebrate holidays. It is in the sacrifice of sharing, but not necessarily preparing, that Christians find the meaning of Christ's sacrifice. This tradition is rooted in religion, but may be endemic. For example, *"to figure out how well two individuals will cooperate with one another, it might help to see if they are able to civilly sit down and share a meal together....[B]onobos are willing to share food with one another, regardless of sex or age"* (Wax, 2007). Even in mixed groups, sharing food sacrifices differences, long held as comforts, in favor of open dialogue and growing new traditions. The symbolism of food is evident in Mexican-Filipino relations in California (Brown, 2014; Wirpsa, 1998). *"Unity"* is *"needed, especially in Los Angeles"* (Wirpsa, 1998, p. 3). *"Filipinos are in a special position, because of language and culture, to be bridge-builders....Filipinos have a special affinity...with Mexican Catholics because of history: In 1521, the Spaniards came via Mexico to the 7,107 islands that make up the Philippines"* (Wirpsa, 1998, p. 3). Spaniards were present in the Philippines for 400 years. Filipino culture is rooted in Christianity, and represents the largest community of Catholics in Asia.

Filipinos represent the largest Catholic population in Asia; 400 years of Spanish presence in the country rooted Christianity deeply in the lives of the people. Most Filipinos in Los Angeles identify as Catholic. One connection between Filipinos and Mexican holiday pageantry is their shared mixed heritage. Tribal Filipinos and Native Americans deified elements and earthly substances, celebrated agriculture, danced, and made ritual sacrifices. On both continents, tribal heritage transformed the expression and symbolism of Christian holidays. Their shared home, Los Angeles, bridges language barriers. *"The culture of the Spaniards had been transformed in Mexico and was transformed again in the Philippines"* (Wirpsa, 1998, p. 3). Similar to the Americas, diverse indigenous cultures of tribal people thrived "*in the Southeast Asian archipelago at the time of the Spanish invasion. Filipinos today speak 87 languages and dialects that survived from ancestral origins of 111 Malay, Indonesian and mainland Asian cultural and linguistic groups"* (Wirpsa, 1998, p. 3). Many speak English with Mexicans in the United States. Filipinos are committed to their holidays, which involve milkfish, onions, ginger, garlic, spicy catfish in broth, spaghetti, garlic bread, and other dishes and flavors. They may sing and stomp rhythmically; and eat from *"huge tray[s] stacked with saping saping, a thick, gooey rice dessert of three tiers of color"* (Wirpsa, 1998, p. 3). One Filipino said, *"We don't want [these customs] to die. This is why we are trying to teach the youth"* (Wirpsa, 1998, p. 3). Another specified that *"it is important that Filipino youth be raised in the Christian life"* (Wirpsa, 1998, p. 3). *"The children will be given a good foundation...when they mingle with different people in different ways....[E]ven if they mix with many kinds of people, they are strong"* (Wirpsa, 1998, p. 3). Their mixed group is *"like a family"* with *"brothers and sisters. My other friends...want to have fun,...here we know what's right and wrong"* (Wirpsa, 1998, p. 3). *"[S]haring...help[s] bring in a multicultural parish"* (Wirpsa, 1998, p. 3). *"Spirituality is our individual way of experiencing our relationship with God....We are born in different places at different times. I don't think God expects us to express our faith in just one mode"* (Wirpsa, 1998, p. 3). *"[W]hat I've been through as a"* member of a *"race, a people, [and] a nation,"* causes you to *"feel much more comfortable in your relationship with God [and] expressing yourself in that way. It's something"* that is *"part of being born and reared in that culture"* (Wirpsa, 1998, p. 3). Cultural undertones and festivities link groups of people to their Christian faith.

The Eucharist, a pancontinental symbol of sharing, *"memorializes Jesus' sacrifice"* (Martens, 2014, p. 47). *"[T]he ancient types"* of food, such as bread and fish, *"point to spiritual fulfilment"* (Martens, 2014, p. 47). Presently, Biblical and religious scholars concentrate *"on the literal sense of Scripture and do not minimize the reality of the Israelite experience, which itself was true physical and spiritual nourishment"* (Martens, 2014, p. 47). However, scholars view Jesus' *"interpretation"* of manna *"as a type of the bread of heaven. The food of the Eucharist, therefore, recalls the manna in the wilderness, creates unity and points"* Christians to *"true spiritual homeland"* (Martens, 2014, p. 47). *"Like the memory of the Israelite salvation from captivity, which is memorialized at Passover, so in the Eucharist, Jesus' own sacrifice is memorialized in the life of the church"* (Martens, 2014, p. 47). When Christians *"break bread," "[t]he Eucharist becomes a source of memory"* (Martens, 2014, p. 47). Christians *"do not divide the body but participate in a sign of unity: 'Because the loaf of bread is one, we, though many, are one body.' This sharing has an ecclesial aspect"* (Martens, 2014, p. 47).

The bread is a Eucharistic sign and *"foretaste of the Messianic banquet"* (Martens, 2014, p. 47). The Eucharist is related to Moses' search for the promise land. It is connected to Jews' deep appreciation for food as a harvest, celebration, commemoration, and means for sharing. *"Some of"* the *"most potent Jewish memories involve food. Food memories go very deep. In the hollow of one spoon filled with chicken soup,"* Jews *"may be transported to" "the sounds, tastes and smells of family that emerge from sanctifying the basic primal need to eat"* (Kurlander & Rakitt, 2013). "*Nowhere is the connection between food and"* sharing *"stronger than at the [S]eder table"* (Kurlander & Rakitt, 2013). Jews *"are joined to the people around the table by profound bonds of history"* (Kurlander & Rakitt, 2013). *"The coincidence of the dates of Ramadan,"* November 17 through December 17, *"to the Christian observance of Advent"* December 2 through December 25, *"as well as key Jewish holy days such as Hanukkah,* December 10 through December 17 demonstrates togetherness (*National Catholic Reporter,* 2001). They *"have the salt water representing the tears" "and the charoset signaling the cement"* (*National Catholic Reporter,* 2001). Jews, like Santeros, Hindus, Buddhists, and other religious practitioners share food with nonexistent people. During Passover, Jews *"pour a cup of wine for Elijah..., inviting a mysterious figure...to be metaphorically present"* (Kurlander & Rakitt, 2013). *"Food is a way" that they "nurture and demonstrate love for others"* (Kurlander & Rakitt, 2013). Jews, like Christians, *"believe that one great way to reach out to others is to extend a hand in friendship across a table, to share a meal that can help us share a story"* (Kurlander & Rakitt, 2013). However, *"crisis has also forced to the surface an urgent, shared desire worldwide among ordinary people of goodwill"* quickly to *"build bridges of understanding between cultures,"* religions, and societies (Kurlander & Rakitt, 2013). *"The beliefs and energies of those traditions might offer the only hope for resolving conflict before it spirals out of control in what some suggest is the intended and ultimate terrorist act, to precipitate an explosion of hatred between major world religions"* (Kurlander & Rakitt, 2013). *"In [B]iblical terms, the threat we face together" "can be confronted only by prayer and fasting"* (Kurlander & Rakitt, 2013). A festival for fasting, Ramadan, *"is impressive in its potential to marshal spiritual discipline and power to create an enormous community of purpose. Christians might take note and be inspired to share in so mighty a prayer for justice for the poor and hungry"* (*National Catholic Reporter,* 2001). *"Imagine the world that could emerge beyond our present terror if"* everyone *"joined to pray and fast together"* (*National Catholic Reporter,* 2001). The possibility is not untenable particularly because some holy days overlap.

Muslims and Mennonites shared an interfaith potluck (Chin, 2011). A Mennonite pastor blessed the food, while Muslims shared stories about their lives and described their faith. The Mennonites talked about Christianity as a community and their faith at the event where both groups were equally represented. They shared halal, vegetarian, and non-halal food (Chin, 2011; Cusack, 2011). They discussed Jesus as a significant historical and spiritual leader, and Muslims emphasized the importance of building friendships.

When people lack food, Christians may bond by sharing their food with them (Ellis, 2014). Homeless outreach and community donations to homeless individuals and families are common; however, the government regulates these activities and has banned groups from freely using public areas to provide food to the homeless or they implement particular safety regulations. Regulations have discouraged, deterred, or resulted in sanctions against some Christians who have refused to change their longstanding programs. *"Every meal" "is an opportunity to consider the theology of food, and all bread shared is God shared. Eating anything, from mole to Eucharist to 'our daily bread,' is an act imbued with both theological and political meaning"* (Frykholm, 2010, p. 40). *"God offers" "nourishment, even the nourishment of God's self"* (Frykholm, 2010, p. 40). This means that Christians may be able to share with homeless individuals without breaking the law by nurturing their souls; however, they may lose the opportunity to bond by sacrificing food. Sharing food is a sacrificial *"gesture to others"* (Frykholm, 2010, p. 40). *"Unlike other theologies in which God's gift can never be reciprocated," "a divine economy in which there is an implicit return in giving"* may not be the same as one that scarifies the body's desires (Frykholm, 2010, p. 40). When two people share food with each other, *"[t]he reciprocal gesture is never identical to the gift, and the gift can never be measured precisely, but in giving, God also receives. God's desire is both satisfied and ongoing"* (Frykholm, 2010, p. 40). There is *"divine economy by sharing our own daily bread and inviting others to the divine feast"* (Frykholm, 2010, p. 40). It is in sharing that the act of nourishment is accomplished on a spiritual level.

One religious scholar described how she addressed a group by using the meaning of fish derived from her childhood memories of Christmas as a guiding metaphor (O'Sullivan, 2003). "*In the preVatican II era, Christmas Eve was a day of abstinence, meaning we usually had a major meal that included fish and no meat"* (Felton 2006). She said, "*I continued the fish theme by relating how we had to 'fish' for our Christmas gifts because my grandmother did not put to-and-from tags on our presents"* (Felton 2006). *"I ended my story with a reflection on Jesus' promise to make the Apostles fishers of people who would grow strong in the faith and live in the joy of the Kingdom of God"* (Felton 2006). In some cultures, traditions live on, but symbolism is only recognized externally by scholars and tourists. Emphasizing sacrifice allows families to share holidays by developing freshly made syncretic holiday feasts dressed in old world tradition (Edinborough, 1987; Hofman, 2003).

Chapter 15

Book of Tobit

The Book of Tobit shares thematic elements with the story of Jonah. Like Jonah, Tobit faces Nineveh's destruction. After concealing his identity and hiding in the belly of the ship, Jonah identifies himself as the cause of the storm and volunteers to be thrown overboard into the sea. Like Tobit, Jonah begs God to let him die through his misfortunate trials. After being attacked by a large aquatic animal, each protagonist comes into closer proximity with the animal's internal organs.

Jonah is not the only liar. Christians may lie routinely to be better Christians, for example put on a brave face to seem happy and blessed. This testimonial is made with good intentions. *Christianity Today* declared that Christians often lie in the following seven ways: 1) When they *"claim"* that they *"are more confident than"* they *"really are;"* 2) *"claim that unexplainable things are in fact explainable;"* 3) "*don't acknowledge" "doubts within the drama of faith;"* 4) *"pretend like the Bible doesn't say some really nasty things when" "it does;"* 5) *"claim"* theologically to *"understand other beliefs, faiths and world views"* that they have not experienced or studied; 6) "*claim that all of"* their *"beliefs are"* infallible; "and 7) "*pretend like"* they "*really love the other person when"* they do not (Kriz, 2014). These lies are evident in Jesus' actions; for example, when he turned water into wine; multiplied the loaves and fishes; and taught his followers to turn the other cheek. Misleading suggestions are evident in Jesus' actions, including the suggestion that Jesus would prefer followers to choose overindulgence in wine, a sacrament, rather than consume water, an element of baptism; Jesus will end world hunger; and one may be content with being slapped or complacently witness another get slapped. In some regards, Jesus' crucifixion was a charade. He disclosed his intention to rise from the dead, and needed publicly to be crucified to prove that he could rise from the dead; however, his methodology was part of God's will that devised the means to his end. The resurrection is similar to a fixed bout. God invented the terms of the game; created rules that allowed Jesus to win; claimed that any believer could rise; and publicly demonstrated the unlikelihood that mere mortals could resurrect. Jesus was bound to his roles as a Jewish rabbi and human; and therefore, God's charade may have been necessary. This may be the same reason why Christians lie.

Like Jesus, Tobit's son Tobiah is sent by Tobit to marry a bride, Sarah, who is suffused with death. Sarah was married seven times previously, but a demon, Asmodeus, killed her husbands before the marriages were consummated. Immediately before meeting Sarah, Tobit is attacked by a large fish, but he is unharmed. He is able to capture and dismember the fish. An angel tells him to safely preserve the heart, gall, and liver, which can be used to exercise demons (Novick, 2007). Fish hearts and livers were used with ashes and burnt perfumes to fumigate evil spirits early in Israel's history (Goodhugh & Taylor, 1943). They burn the heart and liver as an incense to cleanse Sarah of the demon so that she can marry Tobiah. Tobiah's wife Sarah foreshadows both the Christian church and Mary Magdalen, who is believed by contemporary Christians to have been a prostitute and appears to be one of the only women travelling with Jesus and his disciples, none of whom were married to Mary (Luke 7:36-50; Machiela & Perrin, 2014; Van Den Eynde, 2005). Tobit believes that he is doing God's work when he sends his son into a marriage that may kill him. However, in the morning Tobiah is found sleeping with Sarah, which proves that Asmodeus had been exercised (Goldfeder & Sheff, 2013). Christians *"cannot help but recognize this fish as a solution corresponding to the problems that occasioned Tobit's and Sarah's prayers"* (Schellenberg, 2011, p. 317). The gall is used later to heal Tobit of blindness.

Omission, concealment, and deflection may be forms of lying. Lying is a violation of the Ten Commandments. The Book of Tobit was written before Christ. The Book of Tobit's most widely recognized depiction was written after the Ten Commandments and likely after Abraham's covenant. God's angel lies repeatedly to Tobit (Miller, 2012). He is the only angel overtly to lie in the New or Old Testaments. This may indicate that the Ten Commandments are intended for humans to follow, and are not universal rules. Because the angel lies, readers see that God is capable of lying, and therefore the Ten Commandments do not apply to God. *"The only angel to lie is Raphael in the Book of Tobit, masquerading as an Israelite named Azariah who claims to be Tobit's kinsman (5:5,13). At first glance, the angel utters a 'white lie' about his name and background without causing any harm to those beguiled"* (Miller, 2012, p. 492). The angel's *"prevarication seems permissible in that he eventually reveals his identity later in the tale (12:15). When one reads the text more carefully," "it becomes evident that Raphael lies repeatedly in the story"* (Miller, 2012, p. 492).

Some scholars accept the Book of Tobit as a completely *"fictional novel"* formed in approximately 200 B.C.E. (Miller, 2012, p. 493). The analysis may not be congruent with ethical and moral evaluations of other books, such as the Gospels, which are believed by many Christians to be literal and historical facts (Miller, 2012, p. 493). In some purviews, Tobit's angel, Raphael, does not lie. He misleads Tobit on minor issues for his own good. In law, this may be similar to puffing or misrepresentation of immaterial facts (Cusack, 2016). *"Then again, perhaps Raphael is not lying. When the angel claims in 5:13 that he is Azariah, son of Hananiah, his statement"* is basically true, *"for these epithets symbolically convey the truth about his mission and purpose"* (Miller, 2012, p. 495). *"Raphael's mendacity"* may demonstrate *"his role"* as a liar and a purist (Miller, 2012, p. 499). Book of Tobit does not denote God's command for Raphael to be deceitful; yet, *"God's tacit approval is plausible"* (Miller, 2012, p. 500). God is not known to have *"allowed or encouraged previous"* prophets, angels, or heralds to fib (Miller, 2012, p. 500). Furthermore, the angel seems intent on testing Tobit; but, this situation does not seem to require repetitive lies. His mission is critical; however, it has terrestrial and spiritual ramifications, which seem to imply that truthfulness is essential. *"He is assigned a critical mission that has ramifications not only in the human arena but also in the spiritual realm. Besides curing Tobit's blindness and joining Tobiah and Sarah in marriage, he must also subdue the demon Asmodeus, showing that"* his instructions from God were accurate (Miller, 2012, p. 500).

The story may be viewed as fiction or excluded from the King James Bible, not only because God's angel lies, but also because of negative allusions to Jesus. "*Tobit is a negligent father who sends his only son on a perilous journey with a man,*" *"who claims without proof to be related to him"* (Miller, 2012, p. 505). The man *"claims without proof to know the way,"* and "*gives false assurances about the safety of a route that Tobit knows full well is dangerous"* (Miller, 2012, p. 505). Tobit is a failure because he neglects to think about Tobiah's "*welfare because he allows himself to be distracted by peripheral matters: the money he left with Gabael and Raphael's genealogical pedigree"* (Miller, 2012, p. 505). Tobit's persistent attention to money is apparent at the conclusion of Chapter Four and opening of Chapter Five. Tobit "*tells his son about ten talents of silver he deposited with Gabael"* (Miller, 2012, p. 505). Tobit directly makes six remarks about money, wages, wealth, and poverty in five verses spanning Tobit 4:20 and Tobit 5:3. However, his reticence to prioritize his son's safety is evident because "*he mentions only once that his son should find a trustworthy...guide"* (Miller, 2012, p. 505). *"The emphasis should have been the other way around, but money is at the forefront of his mind and has impaired his judgment. Tobit's judgment is clouded also by his fixation on proper lineage"* (Miller, 2012, p. 505). Tobit may cause readers to view Jesus' mission as being flawed because the premise of his presence on Earth is both truthful and pretentious. Perhaps Jesus misleads as a result of environmental conditions, for example he was given to humanity by an all loving God, who willfully tortures his only son to prove his love.

The story may allude to Tobit's wife as being a Mother-God. "*Responsible parenthood is demonstrated instead by Anna, who serves as a foil to her husband in this episode. Tobit does not have his priorities straight, and his wife's rebuke highlights his oversight"* (Miller, 2012, p. 506). Some scholars may argue that she would happily dwell in an impoverished condition beside her husband so long as Tobiah is protected. She says, "*Don't let money come first! Rather let it be a ransom for our son! What the Lord has given us to live on is certainly enough for us*" (Tobit 5:19-20). Tobit may be understood as a patriarch. He is seeing impaired, but will receive a miracle even though he compromises his son's safety (Miller, 2012, p. 506). She is a Mother-God character because she is temperate and forsakes excess to secure her son's safety. *"Tobit could benefit from his wife's advice, not only because she puts family and money in proper perspective but also because she trusts in God's providence, something Tobit failed to accept earlier. But Tobit will not listen to her,"* and "*does he recognize the angel's tests"* (Miller, 2012, p. 506). With the omission of a Mother-God's techniques and skills, humans become subject to humans after creation by God the Father (Cousland, 2003). Despite the omissions implicating the Torah (i.e. Pentateuch), Book of Tobit is about a sojourner's obedience (Machiela & Perrin, 2014; USCCB, 2016; Van Den Eynde, 2005).

Chapter 16

Christian art

Christian music, films, plays, and paintings consistently use fish to communicate Christian metaphors and messages. Orthodox, conservative, reform, and mystical sects of Judaism may compare fish to "*souls awaiting salvation*" (Duncan & Derret, 1980, p. 109). Some believe that fish are reincarnated souls. Fishermen utilizing lines and nets may be analogized to or symbolize "*God's agents effectuating that salvation*" (Duncan & Derret, 1980, p. 109). The objects that may seem to vivify literary narratives actually "*articulate*" a *"prophecy"* (Duncan & Derret, 1980, p. 109). Fishing and fishermen in the stories are literally and figuratively similar to present-day "*agents of the coming of God's reign, preparing (odd as it may seem) for the Banquet at which the fish will be diners, not dish*" (Duncan & Derret, 1980, p. 109). Rediscovering and performing traditions of thought and ritual frame art "*in an entirely new light*" (Duncan & Derret, 1980, p. 109).

The revelation begins with adherents, but extends to their places of worship. *"Churches are like arks with stained glass windows recreating the rainbow, and from Noah's point of view, projecting the world to come from his family's survival and covenant with God"* (Down, 2005). It includes literature, such as *Moby Dick,* and may include archeologically relevant works of art, such as cave paintings in the New World; but, metaphoric revelations and Christian expression may be most valuable in the form of fine art and literature (Melville, 1999). D. H. Lawrence asked, *"What then is Moby Dick*" (Lawrence, 1917; Melville, 1999)*?* Lawrence concluded, *"He is the deepest blood-being of the [W]hite race; he is our deepest blood-nature"* (Lawrence, 1917). Lawrence transcends his body, and his awareness of his inner conflict, compassionately to observe whale slaughter. *"There is something really overwhelming in these whalehunts, almost superhuman or inhuman, bigger than life"* (Lawrence, 1917). As he reenters his own mind to analyze his own perceptions, he focuses on the protagonist, viewed by Ahab as the antagonist. "*[H]e is hunted, hunted, hunted by the maniacal fanaticism of our [W]hite mental consciousness. We want to hunt him down"* (Lawrence, 1917). Lawrence believes that *Moby Dick* is about subjugation of Whiteness through a *"maniacal conscious hunt of ourselves"* (Lawrence, 1917; Melville, 1999). Lawrence believes that social contracts with and recruitment of *"dark races," "pale,"* non-Whites*, "[R]ed, [Y]ellow, and [B]lack,"* races, people from the *"east and west,"* and religious minorities, such as *the "Quaker and fireworshipper" "help us in this ghastly maniacal hunt which is our doom and our suicide"* because only through self-destruction can White people see themselves as part of it *"all"* (Lawrence, 1917).

Lawrence groups together all White people. Lawrence does not distinguish males and females, but implicitly classifies White females with White males, not with other minorities. He neglects tingism that carefully segregates White people according to tinge; for example, White Hispanics from White non-Hispanics; beige, pink, tan, or fair skin; and platinum, ash blonde, or wheat-colored (tow) hair. Tingism is a screen for inner-racial bias. The ostensible matrix lacks methodological foundations for observing differences, defining classifications, or determining analytical relevance. Due to globalization and inherent differences between nationals from the same European countries and diasporas, many preformulated conceptions about tinge and race are specious. They may be *a priori* attempts to guard against rejection and tension; but, they often fail to excavate any reliable data indicating nation of origin or people's predispositions to deviate from alleged local culture holding itself to be a ubiquitous maxim and faction of White society.

Lawrence insults the relationship between White humans (e.g. European Americans) and Quakers. He is aware that even Christian minorities are outsiders. They are not directly attacked by White consciousness, and may lack awareness of the majority's inner struggles, even though they may feel subjected to political unfairness ensuing from inner conflict. The conflict may result from repressed differences among White humans. Thousands of years of war, enslavement, and conquest between Europeans and diasporas has been sublimated by globalization, Americanization, imperialism, and political correctness. Whitewashing in America and cultural mixing at work and home may exacerbate latent, repressed, and ignored tensions that become internalized self-rejection. The social goal becomes conformity to a pretentious group ethos rather than participation in an expressive homogenous culture. National and local homogeneity is a basis for Europeans' particular traditions and mentalities. Lawrence's analysis hides deep struggles between European peoples. To accept their prefabricated role as a majority in America, Americans with European ancestors may identify as Caucasian (e.g. Slavic), Anglo (e.g. British), Saxon (e.g. German), or other appropriated or externally imposed labels taken for granted by outsiders as homogenous, flexible, or monolithic "racial" classifications applicable to all White people. *"The last phallic being of the [W]hite man. Hunted into the death of upper consciousness and the ideal will. Our blood-self subjected to our will"* (Lawrence, 1917).

Lawrence stands by his conscious desire for destruction when he concludes that the Redeemer could be viewed as a whale. "*To use the words of Jesus, IT IS FINISHED....Consummatum est! Post-mortem effects, presumably. Because, in the first centuries, Jesus was Cetus, the Whale. And the Christians were the little fishes. Jesus, the Redeemer, was Cetus, Leviathan. And all the Christians all his little fishes*" (Lawrence, 1917).

Melville's tale incorporated whaling customs of the day. Their ambiguity demonstrated inner conflict and absence of standardized protocols attested to their distinct cultural backgrounds. However, their willingness to follow the fast-fish, loose-fish rules alleviated violent conflicts and alluded to similar broad understandings of justice and general welfare.

According to Melville, whalemen from America were *pro se* litigants, who also mediated and judged their own claims using fast-fish, loose-fish rules (Deal, 2009, p. 200). Their system of informal judgement lacked statutes, ordinances, courts, judicial opinions, legislatures, law enforcement, and *stare decisis.* They employed their own rules and enforced customs. "*The universal law that prevented such 'vexatious and violent disputes' was reduced by Melville to a pair of pithy maxims. 'I. A Fast Fish belongs to the party fast to it. II. A Loose-Fish is fair game for anybody who can soonest catch it'*" (Deal, 2009, p. 200). *"Like most attempts at brevity and concision in the law, Melville's summation raised more questions than it answered haling dispute is well illustrated by the 1808 Common Pleas decision in Fennings v. Lord Grenville"* (Deal, 2009, p. 200).

Melville may have elucidated the conflict once again by setting his story, *The Encantadas,* in the Galapagos Islands (Melville, 2005). Rigid customs theoretically encourage flexible application. Enduring rituals and behavior codes are respected by partakers. Pressure to abide by customs results from participants' desires to be peaceable within their community. Submission to makeshift tribunals is unlike deterrence and obedience resulting from fear of state sanctioned consequences. Like judges and jurors in England in the 1800s, groups of whalemen may carefully have analogized and distinguished precedence to achieve results that reflected group values rather than consistent judgments. Consistency may equate with fairness expected from courts, but fairness in makeshift panels may correlate with perception, professional patterns, entitlement, and other factors. Courts that heard whalemen's cases may have applied precedents that were foreign or unfair to both parties accustomed informally to settling disputes. This threat may have further enforced customary rules between whalemen (Deal, 2009).

Some courts were guided by whalemen's customs. In *Fennings v. Lord Grenville,* two English whaling ships, the William Fennings and the Caerwent, disputed the rules in Galapagos Islands (Deal, 2009). The William Fennings struck a second whale in the course of killing the primary target. The whale did not immediately die, but it was slowed by a buoy attached by the William Fennings. The Caerwent killed the whale. Under the fast-fish lose-fish rules, obeyed in Greenland fisheries, the Caerwent could possess the whale because the loose whale was unattached to the William Fennings. Whalers in the Galapagos Islands utilized the custom of awarding one half of the whale to each party. *"Judge Chambre advanced in his concurrence the importance of following custom in an area of commerce engaged in by the subjects of many nations. Failure to abide by established customs would result in a sort of warfare between ships that might eventually extend to the nations of those involved"* (Deal, 2009, p. 222). Melville's perception of cultural tensions may call readers' unconscious attention to their own inner conflicts in order to prey on their vulnerabilities and captivate them.

The importance of food, feasting, and harvesting to the Israelites' continues to be evident in Jewish holidays. The importance is stressed in the New Testament, but may be overlooked in Christian art. *"Alas, there is a serious misunderstanding relative to the fish"* (Duncan & Derret, 1980, p. 118). Christian religious knowledge *"projects the symbolic fish, ubiquitous in Jewish art, as eucharistic food"* (Duncan & Derret, 1980, p. 118). The relationship between Jewish art, food, and Christian art, therefore, is vicarious. *"Implausible enough in any case, this must be a development of the gospel"* stories to be authentically Christian without focusing on Jewish holidays (Duncan & Derret, 1980, p. 118). *"In fact the explanation of the frequency of fish in Jewish as also Christian catacombs, tombs, lamps, etc., is simple. As [scholars] have seen, the fish"* embodies historical, cultural, and spiritual connections between life on Earth before and after Christ, but fails to say enough about Christian life (Duncan & Derret, 1980, p. 118).

Christians may attempt to fill-in or replace Jewish expressions about fish by depicting apocalyptic scenes with fish. This directly and indirectly moves Christianity from and toward Jewish beliefs; and therefore, orients itself according to Judaism. For example, a painting may depict that *"[t]he waters of the Last Days have reached, or will reach the soul of the departed, and the sign of the fish anticipates this faith. No doubt other uses of the idea 'fish' are found in rabbinical sources but they are few, marginal, and only decorative"* (Duncan & Derret, 1980, p. 119). Abundant evidence demonstrates that fish symbolically portray immortality. Apocalyptic depictions of fish, for example stained glass scenes, mirror synagogues. Figures of fish meaningfully and prominently decorate synagogues at Beth Alpha in Palestine and Hammam Lif in Tunisia. The fish are not relentlessly swimming in water. They are visualized as having been caught. *"Immediately before the first Redemption the Israelites were like a draught of fish"* (Duncan & Derret, 1980, p. 119).

Christians do not ignore the "*reference to immortality*" (Duncan & Derret, 1980, p. 119). *"It is not surprising that fish figured as amulets in Palestinian graves and with ossuaries"* (Duncan & Derret, 1980, p. 119). Modern Christians may trace symbolism to ancient beginnings; and ancient Christians certainly envisioned that their symbolism would endure, *ergo* immortality. *"The fish caught with a rope will not be a fish for food! It is a symbol of the individually saved soul (the myth of Orpheus and pagan tomb-art quite apart). This does not exclude the symbol of the net, but is more suitable...for individual interments!"* (Duncan & Derret, 1980, p. 119). *"Apart from the sculptured or painted fish, and the tendentious translations," "the beautiful and deliberate use of [Ezekiel] xlvii g-rr at Babylonian Talmud, lVI. Q., 25b" "[i]n a memorial poem by Bar Qipoq about R. Ashi the fish corresponds to the righteous man, while lesser persons are indicated by the marshes. The righteous are fished out by the fishermen as Leviathan will be fished"* (Duncan & Derret, 1980, p. 120). *"That [Ezekiel] xlvii lies in the background to the Calling of the Apostles is [recognized] in some places in early Christian literature and by several theologians of past ages. But it has been forgotten"* (Duncan & Derret, 1980, p. 120). However, in scenes where marshes represent the undesirable, artists may compassionately indicate that these people are not permanently condemned.

Catacomb of the Callixtus is the earliest official cemetery of the Christian community in Rome, Italy (Jensen, 1998). Large magnificent paintings and artistic trims are depicted throughout underground chambers and subterranean cubicles. Scenes include the whale expectorating Jonah, Jesus' baptism, the grave spewing forth Lazarus, and other mythological expressions of hope for redemption, resurrection, birth, and afterlife. Catacombs, ancient sarcophagi, and objects (e.g. lamps) often display painted depictions of Jonah and the whale. "*In the thirteenth century glass of Bourges Cathedral Jonah's deliverance is depicted as one of the types of the Resurrection. This symbolism, of course, found its origin in Our Lord's words"* (Collins, 1913, p. 101). Jesus said, "*As Jonah was three days and three nights in the whale's belly, so shall the Son of Man be three days and three nights in the heart of the earth"* (Matthew 12:40). "*At Bourges Jonah is represented together with other types of the Resurrection, such as the raising of Jairus daughter"* and "*the Pelican in her piety"* (Collins, 1913, p. 101).

Banquet scenes, for example depicting youth around a table, are typical funerary scenes in Christian art. The earliest Christian images depict paradise. Feasting is a symbol for and earthly embodiment of paradise. Banquet scenes in the Sacrament Chambers in Rome may unambiguously promise believers abundance and satisfaction. They are enigmatic because inside the catacombs they do not inspire believers to become fishers of souls; rather they reinforce the purpose of having lived as a Christian. Christians are promised that their sins will be forgiven and they will have prosperity in the afterlife. This promised may be accepted in exchange for their obedience to Jesus, who asks them to be a lamp unto the world and fishers of men. Semicircular and long rectangular banquet tables "break the fourth wall" so that viewers share the feast and are recognized by the subjects of the paintings. This recognition contrasts with the disciples inability to recognize Jesus before the miraculous catch after his resurrection.

Ample baskets of bread, cups of wine, and strategically designed platters of one or two fish indicate how the feast might feel to an adherent (Jensen, 1998). Two fish may signify duality, for example life and death, sustenance and feasting, or Mary and Jesus; whereas a single fish may represent Jesus, eternity, or monotheism. A three-legged table symbolizing, body, spirit, and soul, the trinity, life, death, and resurrection, and other Christian themes may support the fish as they are blessed and offered by a host. Women and men may extend their arms in prayer, to communicate, or to express their feelings. Women may break bread. Bread may be round and marked with a Greek letter "X" symbolizing Christ. These loaves may appear on the table. Commemorating Jesus' miracle of feeding the multitude as a testament to his ability and willingness to provide an endless joyful banquet in the afterlife, scenes may depict two fish, and bread baskets may typically contain five or seven loaves; however, they occasionally may contain six, eight, and ten loaves (Luke 9:10-17; Luke 14:15; Mark 6:30-44, 8:1-10, 14-20, 14:25; Matthew 14:13-21, 15:32-39). No historical evidence of Eucharistic menus proves that these meals were associated with or depicted religious rituals, and therefore, may completely have been symbolic depictions of Jesus' promise and embodiment. In either case, fish was considered to be part of a special, if not sacred, diet.

Figuratively and literally, fish were associated with might, and therefore appear more frequently in paintings than bread and wine (Jensen, 1998). Table scenes frequently depict seven men or youths, which suggests that a banquet of fish will be the miraculous element, whereas bread may be bountiful on Earth and in heaven. Seven disciples were present after the miraculous catch when Jesus roasted fish and provided bread for breakfast following his resurrection (Cusack, 2012). The smoked fish may allude to docetist representations that Jesus' body did not suffer. Yet, the smoked fish suggest that he defeated hell with his sacrifice because burnt fish organs had been used by Jews to exercise demons. Early Christian sarcophagi reliefs and wall paintings illustrate Jesus multiplying bread. Feast scenes do not depict Jesus pointing a wand to multiply bread. The third dimension present in the sarcophagi relief may suggest that bread can be abundant on Earth for Christians.

Greek and Roman funerary iconography represented pagan culture, which was adopted by Christians' religious motifs (Jensen, 1998). For example, Endymion, lover of the moon goddess, was interpreted as Jonah lying under the shade plant before a worm attacked the plant, which withered; and Orpheus, who with music tamed the animals and stones, was depicted as David. Roman images depict deceased individuals on couches lying down, which was the position in which Romans and contemporaneous Jews may have feasted. Like feast scenes, these scenes may depict on a three-legged table, loaves of bread, wine goblets, and food. Other attendants include the deceased's widow, who may appear as a diner, and servants. Sometimes, seven or five formally dressed diners wearing tunics or togas may indulge in bread, wine, fish, and, occasionally meat. The meat may be added to emphasize the specialness of the fish. I Corinthians 15:39 says, *"All flesh is not the same flesh, but there is one kind of flesh of men, another flesh of beasts, another of fish, and another of birds"* (Collins, 1913). Similarly, depictions of lambs may suggest Christ (Collins, 1913). Images of lambs held by Christ denote Christ's flock, Abraham's covenant, or King David, Jesus' ancestor. The same relationship may not be as common in depictions of schools of fish. Although fish represent souls, and Christ may be depicted as a fish, artists tend not to focus Christian themes on schools of fish, which are distinguishable from harvests. However, three fish may be depicted in a triangle (Collins, 1913). Semicircular or half-moon shaped tables in Roman iconography (i.e. *"stibadium"*) are covered in striped tablecloths, which are incorporated into Christian funerary art (Jensen, 1998). Pagan banquet scenes depict lavish past conduct, not the afterlife. Religious Christian funerary and banquet scenes may have been an adoption of Roman art to compensate for disparate economic classes. This may be one reason that Christians depicted death as being peaceful. Martyrs frequently envisioned paradisiacal afterlife set in a graceful garden inhabited by lovely angels. Pagans and Christians may have held banquets near funerals or graves after one week and two days of mourning, on days of remembrance, and on a deceased relative's birthday. Christians similarly honored martyrs and saints to commemorate their deaths as resurrections. For example, second century pagan and Christian mausoleums and catacombs were uncovered near a mid-third-century banquet hall under the church of San Sebastiano in Rome. Diners feasted under a shelter (i.e. *"tricila"*) that had an open columned porch (i.e. *"loggia"*), which accommodated attendants. Diners may have feasted to honor Saint Peter and Saint Paul.

Memorial meals (i.e. *"refrigeria"*) were held in chambers that seated diners on benches and provided chairs for deceased individual's souls; and tables (i.e. *"mensae"*) had impressed channels to hold food (Jensen, 1998). Sarcophagi had included furrows on lids where food could be placed and tubes for bevvies. Ancient fine and literary art depicts wine, cake, oil, bread, fruit, and eggs being offered to the deceased, whose souls were believed to be present. Some places for food were shaped like fish and sometimes were used to offer fish. Church records indicate that officials eventually attempted to slow graveside banquets because they mirrored pagan traditions. A few Christian epitaphs toast the deceased with good refreshment (i.e. *"refrigerium"*). Yet, Christian rituals may not have correlated with a belief that dead souls were present or able to consume food and libations in the afterlife.

Marine life may have particular meanings in addition to Jesus, resurrection, and eternal life. Carolingian, Byzantine, and Gothic artists may depict apostles as fish even though they were fishers of men (Matthew 4:19; Mulch, 2011). Dolphins symbolize virtues, such as mercy and patience, faithfulness, and resurrection. Sardines may represent humble people, such as peasants, and gratitude. Maidens are interpreted to be saintly when they hold codfish in baskets or buckets. Their symbolism may be dualistic conjuring Madonna-Whore appositions. Depictions of cod may suggest lust or wrongdoing when fish are near soldiers and wealthy men. Sharks may symbolize sin, mortality, and sneakiness. Whales are symbols of willingness, gratitude, faithfulness, compassion, and virtues, like sardines and dolphins. Lore held that whales customarily placed sand on their backs while breeching the surface. Seabirds flying over the whale would pitch seeds onto their backs. From the seeds, trees would sprout. Mistaking whales' backs for islands, mariners would attempt to tie their boats and come ashore. They would climb onto whales, erect tents, and start fires. As whales felt the temperature rise, they would become uncomfortable. Plunging below the surface would cause the ships to sink and drown the mariners. Bestiaries frequently depicted this narrative (Collins, 1913).

The devil is symbolized by the whale and the seamen are human souls. The moral is that when humans err they risk placing faulty trust and faith in devilish lures. "*There is rich cultural flavor in animal symbolism*," for example "*peacocks, salmon, and stags*" *"revere[d]"* *"as teachers, friends, and healers"* (Snyder, 2012). "*[A]nimals can teach us how to live in harmony with nature"* (Snyder, 2012). "*[S]tudying the natural cycles of other life forms imparts understanding of how things work on a fundamental level. Animals are aware of changing seasons: some hibernate until spring, and some migrate seasonally"* (Snyder, 2012). *"Much animal symbolism"* *"is associated with fertility and vitality. Fish, in particular the salmon, symbolize wisdom. A common saying is 'fish is brain food'"* (Snyder, 2012). Associations may be traced to utility and abundance, such as during salmon season.

Fish have been recognized by Christian artists as sources of pigment (Goodhugh & Taylor, 1983). Violet or blue-purple mentioned in the Gospels and Revelation is produced from the purpura of a univalve shell-fish abundant in Phoenicia. *"[T]he small quantity of the"* colored *"juice which each fish contains, and the necessity of using it before the animal dies, makes it impossible to bring it to any regular article of traffic"* (Goodhugh & Taylor, 1983, p. 1113). *"These shells are also found in various parts of the Mediterranean"* (Goodhugh & Taylor, 1983, p. 1113). *"In the seas of the Spanish West Indies" "is found a shell-fish, which perfectly resembles the ancient purpura, and, in all probability, is the very same"* (Goodhugh & Taylor, 1983, p. 1113). They are abundant in the Spring and readily collected. "*[B]y rubbing one against another, they yield a kind of saliva or thick glair, resembling soft wax: but the purple dye is in the throat of the fish, and the finest part is lodged in a little white vein"* (Goodhugh & Taylor, 1983, p. 1113). In the South Sea, knuckle-size sea-snails stuck to stones may be covered during high tide. The sea-snails *"contain a liquor or juice that has the true [color] purple. The [color] is very bright, and so durable, that washing rather increases than diminishes its [luster], nor does it fade or decay by use and wearing"* (Goodhugh & Taylor, 1983, p. 1113). It may be used to dye cotton. A cotton thread is pulled through the fish after a suitable amount of liquor has been expressed. "*[I]t takes and retains the tincture without any farther trouble; but the purple [color] is not discovered [until] the thread is dry, the juice being of a milky [color] at first, but it soon changes into green, and at last settles in a purple"* (Goodhugh & Taylor, 1983, p. 1113). "*The purpura lives on the other fish"* (Goodhugh & Taylor, 1983, p. 1113). It may burrow into the sand, "*and as it lies hid, it thrusts up a pointed tongue, which wounds and kills anything that comes over it"* (Goodhugh & Taylor, 1983, p. 1113). "*[T]hey have not been turned to any economical purpose. In reference to the purple vestment"* (Goodhugh & Taylor, 1983, p. 1113). "*[I]t may be observed, that this was not in the time of Our Lord exclusively a regal [color], as it became afterwards from the usage of the Roman"* rulers and high ranking people (Goodhugh & Taylor, 1983, p. 1113). "*[I]n the parable it is figuratively mentioned as the apparel of a rich man; thus courtiers are styled by the old classical historians, purpurati"* (Goodhugh & Taylor, 1983, p. 1113). *"Various kinds of shell-fish yielding [coloring] rather are found on the shores of British islands, and of France, more particularly in Poitou"* (Goodhugh & Taylor, 1983, p. 1113). Vessels, tools, media, and symbolism combine into a single phenomenon here.

Chapter 17

Mythological creatures

Christians may not tolerate belief in dinosaurs, but they ought to because the Bible discusses creatures, such as sea serpents, dragons, and unicorns (Genesis 1; Exodus 20:11; Isaiah 27:1). Dinosaurs are typically described by scientists as prehistoric animals living hundreds millions of years ago, who died prior to human evolution; but, Christians believe that the Bible describes the creation story as having occurred approximately 6,000 years ago, when creatures were created within six days (U.S. Department of the Interior, 2013). Christians may point to lack of scientific evidence. For example, the most complete skeleton ever discovered allegedly was only 85% intact (Spencer & Griffiths, 2014). Many Christians are aware of the lack of paleontological evidence and experience in discovering dinosaurs.

During the 1820s in England, a rare and previously unrecorded tooth was delivered into the possession of a medical doctor (Lessem, Rowe, & Hammer, n.d.). The tooth may have come from a creature, called iguanodon, who grew in excess of 20 feet. The lizard was depicted as having a large spike on his or her head, which was inaccurate. Far more accurate may have been the placement of the spike at the base of the lizard's shortest digit. Iguanodon is depicted as having been a vegetarian, which may be mostly accurate. Evolutionists may contemplate that iguanodons first lived more than 120 million years in the past, before the Cretaceous period. A record shows that there may be around 2,100 skeletal pieces of all kinds of large lizards, also known as "dinosaurs." This may be an overestimate, and does not indicate how few complete skeletons have been discovered. Skeletons may be preserved by sand dunes or sediment deposits in streams where large lizards died. Yet, small bones (e.g. tail bones) may have floated downstream or been blown downhill. Numerous kinds of dinosaurs are depicted by researchers, who study as single fragment or tooth. Some researchers claim to have more than one dozen good Tyrannosaurus rex skeletons, but only two that they describe as being nearly complete skeletons. This claim is relative. Bones collected from several specimens, replicas, and models are pieced together to form exhibitions in natural history museums. The great majority of museum displays are totally synthetic; and paleontologists atypically handle valuable specimens. Some skeletal remains (e.g. plesiosaurs) are not inconsistent with theories that dinosaurs were sea monsters.

Christians may believe that dinosaurs lived contemporaneously with humans and may still exist. For example, some tourists and missionaries to Africa have reported observing dinosaur footprints; and Christians continue to track alleged dinosaurs through locals' accounts and physical evidence (Gibbons, 2002). Christian development of monster folklore pursuant to missionary work is not atypical. For example, St. Patrick of Ireland was an apostle, who arrived on the Island in 432 A.D. The Irish allegedly worshipped snakes. *"He is known to have been much concerned with the serpent and is supposed to have destroyed it, presumably in this case by converting the Irish to Christianity"* (Hannah, 2006, p. 197). He is known as a dragon slayer. "*It is interesting that the Irish harp, now represented as a beautiful woman with celestial wings, seems originally to have been a dragon with extended foray pinions and a semi-fish or lizard-like extremity"* (Hannah, 2006). Christian legends also depict women (e.g. Virgin Mary), who subdue serpents, perhaps reflecting social, sexual, psychological, cultural, and religious intersections.

Christians may support beliefs that dinosaurs still exist by relying on recent discoveries of ancient species that were believed to be extinct. In 1839, fossils of coelacanths found in layers of rock were first recorded (Lyons, n.d.). By 1938, some evolutionists believed that coelacanths were 400 million years old; and they were convinced that coelacanths were the missing link between fish and amphibians. They were certain that the extinct fish stopped living when the last of the large lizards perished around 70 million years in the past. Theoretical constraints suggested that humans and coelacanths could not have been contemporaries. "*On December 24, 1938, the scientific world was rocked when an unidentified fish five feet long and over 100 pounds was brought to shore in South Africa"* (Lyons, n.d.). A fisherman caught the animal near Madagascar in the Indian Ocean, and called the fish "*the great sea lizard"* (Lyons, n.d.). To the fisherman, the fish's pectoral fins appeared similar to legs. The scientific community was confounded to discover that coelacanths were living in the Indian Ocean. The fish's physical appearance was nearly identical to alleged records of fossils. *"It was as shocking as if a living T. rex had been found. After all, they supposedly became extinct at the same time"* (Lyons, n.d.). Though anomalous, the event was not singular. Since the initial coelacanth was taken from the ocean, hundreds have been fished and observed in their environments. Some have been introduced into aquaculture. For example, "*In 1952, they were seen swimming near the Comoro Islands in the Indian Ocean. Another population was found in 1998 off the coast of Indonesia. Surprisingly, local Indonesian fishermen were quite familiar with this fish, having been catching them for years"* (Lyons, n.d.). Neither local scientists, nor foreign scientists had researched this population. *"This living fossil is a thorn in the side of evolutionists. It makes a mockery of evolutionary dating methods, provides further proof of the myths of missing links, and exposes their 'facts' for what they really are"* (Lyons, n.d.).

Christians believing in creationism may assimilate into their beliefs dinosaurs, such as plesiosaurs. They may point to Biblical descriptions of sea monsters to explain that God created dinosaurs (Isaiah 27:1; Psalms 74:13). In reality *"the facts are not at all like fish on the fishmonger's slab. They are like fish swimming about in a vast and sometimes inaccessible ocean"* (Simpson, 2011). "*[W]hat the historian catches will depend partly on chance, but mainly on what part of the ocean he chooses to fish in and what tackle he chooses to use—these two factors being, of course, determined by the kind of fish he wants to catch"* (Simpson, 2011). Historians are able to select facts to paint a portrait. Facts' significance influence how historians compose an account of the past. They methodically choose facts for the purpose of conjuring a scenario; proving the likelihood of an event; and demonstrating causes and effects. A historian must sequence a "*pattern of rational explanation and interpretation"* (Simpson, 2011). Some Christians may accept the possibility that dinosaurs existed, but due to specious reconstruction techniques, lack of knowledge, and financially profitable human interest in them, dinosaurs have been mythologized into their present rendering.

Christians may understand the image of dinosaurs as having developed through similar psychosocial process as other mythological creatures, for example unicorns. Unicorns may embody sea monsters and dinosaurs for some Christians. Unicorns were believes to be sea dwellers and land animals. This notion developed "*in part because of the existence of sea creatures such as the narwhal, but the basis for the idea was the widespread belief in earlier ages that each animal living on the land had an animal equivalent to it in the sea. Thus there were supposed to be water or sea unicorns"* (South, 1987). Sea unicorns have been diversely described. Common descriptions include appearing to be large fish or whalelike.

The unicorn has been depicted in religious art, for example Hieronymus Bosch's *The Garden of Earthly Delights* produced in the 1500s (South, 1987). Three panels depict stages of the life cycle: creation, procreation, and death. "*Three unicorns appear in the left panel of the painting"* (South, 1987). Their appearance in the left panel may suggest that creation separate from procreation and death is an allusion. Procreation and death are present in creation. Unicorns may be antithetical to Christ in this regard. "*One is a white unicorn that has a horse's body, cloven feet, and a straight horn with spiral twistings; next to the white unicorn is a brownish, deerlike unicorn with a curved horn having rounded knobs on it"* (South, 1987). Their congregation and companionship contrast with "*a water unicorn swimming in a pool in the right foreground"* (South, 1987). Bosch depicts *"a strange-looking, composite animal with a fish's body, a horselike head, and a goatlike beard"* (South, 1987). This water unicorn's complementary apparition is located in the central panel. Life begins in a water womb for humans; sex is wet; and their bodies decompose into liquid after death. "*The central panel has a water unicorn, a large fish with an extremely long horn; and at least four unicorns are among the men and animals circling a pool in the middle of the panel"* (South, 1987). The land unicorns have multiplied, but curiously, the water unicorn has not. This may suggest virginal elements popular in Christian themes. *"The form of one of these unicorns is unclear because his body is hidden"* (South, 1987). Sexualized interpretations of the Biblical description of the Garden of Eden claim that Adam and Eve hid after they had carnal knowledge. "*Another unicorn is a white horse whose horn is lined at regular intervals with short, pointed barbs. A third unicorn has a deerlike body, long, erect ears, a goat's beard, and a horn of great length"* (South, 1987). The final unicorn represents a genetic combination of the second and third unicorns. The unicorn "*has cloven feet, a horselike head and body, and a single horn divided into two antlered branches"* (South, 1987).

Typical Greek and Roman artists did not depict unicorns; however, unicorns later became quintessential symbols of Christian ideology (South, 1987). They were significant for two key reasons. First, unicorns are described in the Bible *"because of uncertainty about the meaning of an animal that is called re'em in the Hebrew but is not clearly identified"* (South, 1987). In the majority of contemporary Bible translations, "*re'em"* means *"wild ox"* because "*scholars now think that by the word re'em was meant the aurochs or Bos primigenius,"* a massive and ferocious wild ox (South, 1987). Between 200 A.D. and 300 A.D., the Old Testament was translated into Greek from Hebrew. This translation, known as Septuagint, lacked clarity about the meaning of the word "*re'em"* (South, 1987). The translation was entered as "*monoceros"* meaning "*one-horned"* (South, 1987). Saint Jerome translated the Bible into Latin in 400 A.D. That version, called Vulgate, translated "*re'em"* as *"rhinoceros"* and "*unicornis"* (South, 1987). *"So it was that the unicorn came to be included in the Bible"* (South, 1987). Strong and fierce unicorns are referenced in eight verses in the King James Bible (Deuteronomy 33:17; Isaiah 34:7; Job 39:9–12; Numbers 23:22, 24:8; Psalms 22:21, 29:6, 92:10) (South, 1987). *"The inclusion of the unicorn in the Bible was sufficient proof to most Christians that"* unicorns *"must exist, and helped give"* unicorns "*important symbolic meanings"* (South, 1987).

Second, unicorns became significant because of their "*inclusion in Physiologus, an allegorical bestiary that was probably written sometime between the second and fourth centuries A.D. Translated into Latin, Arabic, Syriac, and a large number of other languages, Physiologus had immense popularity and deeply influenced literature and art, especially during the Middle Ages"* (South, 1987). *"The lore found in Physiologus was later incorporated into the bestiaries"* (South, 1987). *Physiologus* describes a unicorn as a *"small animal that resembles a young goat and has a horn in the center of his head"* (South, 1987). He is too strong to be captured. Hunters *"take a virgin to a place where unicorns are supposed to be. A unicorn comes to the virgin, becomes submissive to her, and gets into her lap; then he is taken to the palace of the king"* (South, 1987). This story is typically paired with an explanatory passage describing the allegorical meaning. Imaginative Christians may visualize unicorns as symbols of Christ. The horn expresses Christ's power and unity between God the Father and Jesus, his son. The Virgin Mary's presence is clear. The unicorn in her lap may seem Oedipal and incestuous, but may be somewhat similar to the idea of the nursing Madonna. Hints of bestiality, and perhaps reverse bestiality (i.e. "humanophilia"), represent amalgamations of flesh and spirit in the baby Jesus. "*[T]he unicorn's getting into her lap is compared to Christ's entering the womb of the Virgin and taking on human flesh"* (South, 1987). A parallel may be observed between the womb and the tomb, where Christ discarded his shrouds and resurrected his body. An erotic erection symbolized by the horn is not evident because the unicorn submits to the virgin. She remains chaste. "*The smallness of the unicorn is said to represent the humility of the Incarnation of Christ. The early church fathers also compared Christ to the unicorn"* (South, 1987). Unfortunate associations between unicorns and the devil developed in the minds of some Christians. Some early Christians interpreted unicorns as destructive and evil forces. Closemindedness toward unicorns is relative because it may have manifested as consecration and steady faith in other literal dogma; but, may have demonstrated fear of uncommonness, which played a part in the tarnishing of Christianity.

Isidore of Seville, a writer in the Middle Ages, described in *Etymologiae "the unicorn as a fierce animal that can overcome the elephant in combat"* (South, 1987). "*He includes the virgin-capture tale, saying that the unicorn falls asleep after putting his head in the virgin's lap, and that the hunters kill him. The killing of the animal was to become an important part of unicorn lore"* (South, 1987). Most people during the Middle Ages *"unquestionably accepted the unicorn as an actual animal. For any right-thinking Christian, the Bible attested to the unicorn's existence; Physiologus and the bestiaries described the creature, providing symbolic associations with Christ; and many of the encyclopedists such as Bartholomaeus Anglicus included an account of the animal in their works"* (South, 1987). Voyagers from Europe to Asia, for example Marco Polo, claimed to have witnessed unicorns. Polo said that a unicorn in Sumatra did not match the European ideal because it was a large, ugly beast dwelling in the bog and mud. *"This was surely not a creature that would allow itself to be taken by a maiden, and surely no maiden would want to capture such a creature"* (South, 1987). Marco Polo's description was about rhinoceroses. *"[A]lthough the animals he saw did not fit the European conception of the unicorn, he and his readers believed he had seen unicorns"* (South, 1987). Thus, perpetuation of this mythology was founded on misidentification.

Throughout the Renaissance public *"[b]elief in the unicorn remained strong;" "[t]here were more eyewitness accounts of the animal, and he was included in natural histories and books on animals"* (South, 1987). Edward Topsell's *History of Four-Footed Beasts,* published in 1607, confidently claimed that Christians rejecting a belief in unicorns denied God's word. The Bible acknowledges, and therefore proves, that unicorns exist. *"He thinks there are 'divers' beasts with a single horn,"* but they are unlike unicorns because their horns lack "*virtue"* (South, 1987). *"The unicorn is the only one-horned beast whose horn contains medicinal and curative powers"* (South, 1987). The swift unicorn is a solitary animal. The allusion to Christ is evident.

Conclusion

Fish symbolize Christ, a tragic, empowered, wise, liberating, sacrificed, and moral figure, who is God's child. Jesus' message and actions demonstrate that fish may represent Christians and souls; may embody wealth and success; represent hunger and satiation; and illustrate monstrous attributes, such as avoidance, violence, insecurity, and envy. *Fish in the Bible:*

Psychosocial and Cultural Analysis of Contemporary Meanings, Values, and Effects of Christian Symbolism synthesizes Biblical references to fish to conclude that fish fundamentally represent duality. Contemporary Christians view the world in terms of duality, established by Jesus' message and grounded in Biblical narratives and perspectives. For example, Christians emphasize the importance of working in contrast to not working; they value goodness as opposed to evil; they share and denounce greed; and Christians promote honor and sanctity. The story of Jonah elucidates heroism and cowardice. Nets represent heaven and a path to hell. Fish may willingly arrive at their destinies or forcibly answer God's call to act. Being all that one can be suggests alternate courses of action, such as yielding to envy, withering with pride, and harming other souls. Christians raise their children to be a dualized audience of Biblical principles, who see others' points of view as narratives unfold and assertions are made.

During the Biblical era, as well as during contemporary eras, convention and tradition have been challenged by globalization and diversity, as demonstrated by the story of Noah's ark. God's kingdom is diverse, but the path to enter is homogenous. This may explain why Christians' concept of fishermen may complicate their understandings of Biblical themes. While they may view real-life fishermen as poor, they may perceive Jesus' mission as being glamorous; some may see fishermen as being well paid, and yet the Piscatory ring suggests that Christians should remain in the material world, where historically they have been more impoverished than other professionals, subjugated by oppressors, and less affluent than cultural counterparts (e.g. pagan Romans).

Christians must grapple with whom to follow—the captain or the crew. Fishermen must decide between old and new treasure, good and bad catches, and proper courses of navigation. Christians also deal with bias against non-Christians. They may suffer from bias, and thus may be aware of the difficulty caused by bias. Christians attempt to govern others in order to confront their own sense of bias; but, their religious values may interrupt their ability to be a detriment to others on a massive scale. To succeed in conservationism,

Christians must not be vulnerable, but must be judicious. Cultural relativism may hamper their abilities to project their views of judicious use of resources onto other nations, and in some cases, their countrymen.

Destiny and free will are summoned at once by Christians examining the meaning of fish because of their ability to choose which fish to eat, when to eat fish, and how much to consume. Bread is another symbol in the Bible, which offsets fish. By its preponderance, it presupposes fish as an equally important allusion to the kingdom of heaven; however, Jesus makes it clear that he disregards bread as the main temptation and the devil respects that. Bread is life-giving and represents eternal life; yet, Jesus respects fish and does not participate in killing genuine specimens. He may miraculously cause inert, soulless, or dead fish to manifest to satisfy his disciples and the multitudes. Free will is opposed to salvation, which requires obedience. Similarly, liberty is opposed to law, which guards liberty and snuffs it. Paternalistic relationships between law and liberty are evident in thematic representations of Jesus being the same as God in the trinity. Faith is the ultimate dichotomy between believing and not seeing.

In *Fish in the Bible* the Fish Gate symbolizes God's kingdom. Builders and engineers are participatory figures, who transform the meaning of raw materials into a kingdom. They help inaugurate Solomon's knowledge with physical signs of his establishment. They formulate his ideas into solid venues and allow fish to be sold. His subjects are minions, who eat fish, but do not worship them. This is a major difference between Christians and pagans.

Christians' negative opinions of themselves may lead to inadequate self-reflection, which becomes projected onto their estimations of fish. Social differences between Christians and between Christians and non-Christians may provoke them to understand fish differently resulting in tension, which may be expressed socially, economically, and culturally. This tension is foreseeable because it has been occurring for thousands of years. Their pursuit of rewards may be one delimiting factor that precludes them from misunderstanding fish to a degree that disintegrates their working relationships or cultural affinities for fish and fishing.

From Christianity, non-Christians are to learn the symbol of fish. They may choose from several examples, including the disciples, Jesus, and non-Christians in the Bible (e.g. Jonah and Noah). This aggregation of characters may critically engage non-Christians as an invitation into Christianity or may put them off depending on their perspectives. It is this dynamic that is relevant today.

References

16 U.S.C. § 1857 (2010).

(2003, September 10). PETA: Fishing video games linked to violence against fish. *The Brush Back (1),* 15. Retrieved from http://www.thebrushback.com/Archives/petaviolence_full.htm

Agedorn, A. C. & Neyrey, J. H. (1998). 'It was out of envy that they handed Jesus over' (Mark 15:10): The Anatomy of envy and the Gospel of Mark. *Journal for the Study of the New Testament, 69,* 15-56.

Al-Ardhi, F. & Al-Ani, M. (2008). Maternal fish consumption and prenatal methylmercury exposure: A review. *Nutrition & Health, 19*(4), 289-297.

American Psychological Association (APA). (n.d.). Painful shyness. Retrieved from http://www.apa.org/helpcenter/shyness.aspx

Atkinson, C., et al. (2011). Associations between types of dietary fat and fish intake and risk of stroke in the caerphilly prospective study (CaPS). *Public Health, 125*(6), 345-348.

Ayotte v. Planned Parenthood of Northern New England, 546 U.S. 320 (2006).

Baarda, T. (1991). "Chose" or "collected": Concerning an Aramaism in logion 8 of the Gospel of Thomas and the question of independence. *Harvard Theological Review, 84*(4), 373.

Baigell, M. (2013). Biblical narratives in contemporary Jewish American art. *Shofar, 31*(3), 1-24, 220.

Bartlett, S. C. (1879). *From Egypt to Palestine through Sinai, the Wilderness and the South Country.* Franklin Square, NY: Harper & Brothers.

Baum, J. (2014, August 19). *Alaska State Troopers,* Season 6, Episode 6.

Bellotti v. Baird, 428 U.S. 132 (1976).

Bergman, J. (1991). On Davis' "A whale of a tale." *Perspectives on Science & Christian Faith, 43,* 224-237.

Boatright, M. C., Hudson, W. M., & Maxwell, A. (1964). *A Good Tale and a Bonnie Tune.* Denton, TX: University of North Texas.

Bogomolova, V. V., Kozlova, S. L., & Kukharev, N. N. (2014). World leaders in production of fish and fish products. *Proceedings of the Southern Scientific Research Institute of Marine Fisheries and Oceanography, 52,* 164-177.

Break Clips. (2014, August 20). Grouper eats 4ft shark in one bite. Retrieved from https://www.youtube.com/watch?v=J5Tfb_ichVs

Brown, P. (2014, January). Mission dualism. *The Presbyterian Record, 138,* 11-12.

Bumble Bee. (n.d.). Products Related. Retrieved from http://www.bumblebee.com/faqs/products-related/

Burge, G. M. (1998, August). Fishers of fish. *Christian History,* 36.

Burwell v. Hobby Lobby, 573 U.S. ___ (2014).

Butler, B. (2016, September 2). Interview at Gulf Regional Fisheries Training Center. New Orleans, LA.

Cai, J. B. F. (2011). *Jesus the shepherd: A narrative-critical study of Mark 6:30–44* (Order No. 3481896). Available from Religion Database. (908612911).

Cal. Fish & Game Code § 2021 (2014).

--. § 2021.5 (2014).

Camille, A. (2001, June). Who's counting? *U.S. Catholic, 66,* 43-45.

Campbell, J. (2008). *The Hero with A Thousand Faces.* Novato, CA: New World Library.

Cato, J. C. & Sweat, D. E. (2000). Fishing: Florida's first industry. *Florida Keys Sea Heritage Journal, 10*(4), 1, 10-14.

Chin, M. (2011, May 2). Muslims, Mennonites share interfaith potluck for peace. *Canadian Mennonite, 15,* 22.

Clarke, S. (2008). Use of shark fin trade data to estimate historic total shark removals in the Atlantic ocean. *Aquatic Living Resources, 21*(4), 373-381.

Clark, S. L., & Wasserman, J. N. (1980). The soul as salmon: Merswin's "neunfelsenbuch" and the idea of parable. *Colloquia Germanica, 13*(1), 47–56.

Coan, S. M. (2015). The future of zoos and aquariums. *Vital Speeches of the Day, 81*(9), 284.

Collins, A. H. (1913). *Symbolism of Animals and Birds Represented in English Church Architecture.* London, UK: Sir Isaac Pitman & Sons.

Coogan, P. (2016). Superheroes. In *Pop Culture Universe: Icons, Idols, Ideas.* Santa Barbara, CA: ABC-Clio.

Copyright Act of 1976, 17 U.S.C. § 107 (1976).

Corgan, B. (1996). "Zero." *Mellon Collie and the Infinite Sadness.* Hollywood, CA: Virgin Records.

Cotter, P. A., McLean, E., & Craig, S. R. (2009). Designing fish for improved human health status. *Nutrition & Health, 20*(1), 1-9.

Cousland, J. R. C. (2003). Tobit: A comedy in error? *The Catholic Biblical Quarterly, 65*(4), 535-553.

Cowden, J. (1964). *Flipper.* Los Angeles, CA: Metro-Goldwyn-Mayer.

Cusack, C. M. (2009). The humane treatment of animals in compliance with Abrahamic law and morals. Unpublished research. College of Law, Florida International University.

--. (2012). Alternative dispute resolution and niyama, the second limb of yoga sutra, *In Factis Pax, 6,* 107-122.

--. (2012). Death revolution: Eating the dead to save our world. *Journal of Environmental & Animal Law, 4,* 37-72.

--. (2012, July). NOnCOnsensual INsemination (No Coin). Research proposal and discussions. Planned Parenthood of the Great Northwest and Juneau

Pro-Choice Coalition and Political Action Committee. Via e-mail and in-person. Juneau, AK.

--. (2015). *Animals and Criminal Justice.* Piscataway, NJ: Transaction Publishers.

--. (2016). "Cuba nos une": Ending the Cuban Adjustment Act. *Journal Law & Social Deviance, 11,* 1-53.

--. (2017). Double glazed: Reflection, narcissism, and Freudian implications in twincest pornography. *Journal of Law & Social Deviance, 1,* 1-42.

--. (2016). Save the white tiger. *Journal of Law & Social Deviance, 12,* 1-12.

Cusack, C. M. & Telesco, G. (2012). Nonconsensual Insemination: Intimate Partner Violence, Patriarchy, Police Education, and Policy. *Journal of Law & Social Deviance, 4,* 271-320.

Cusack, C. M. & Waranius, M. E. (2015). Visual detection of sex offenders and consequential biases among Christians. *Journal of Law & Social Deviance, 10,* 42-67.

Danbury. (2016, March 31). *Essex Chronicle.*

Deal, R. (2009). Fast-fish, loose-fish: How whalemen, lawyers, and judges created the British property law of whaling. *Ecology Law Quarterly, 37*(1) 199-236.

Derrett, J. D. M. (1977). *Studies in the New Testament: Midrash, Haggadah, and the Character of the Community (vol. 3).* Leiden, The Netherlands: E. J. Brill.

Dickens, C. (2000). Water--the common element: Lessons from antiquity and the health of the environment. *Southern African Journal of Aquatic Sciences,* 253-8.

DiMare, P. C. (2011). *Movies in American History: An Encyclopedia, Volume 1.* Santa Barbara, CA: ABC-CLIO.

Dong, L. (2006). *American Born Chinese.* In *Pop Culture Universe: Icons, Idols, Ideas.* Santa Barbara, CA: ABC-Clio.

Douglas, T. H. (2009). *Inductive preaching with clarity: Qualifying a preacher's employment of Jesus' parable method* (Order No. 3401803). Available from Religion Database. (205437088).

Down, T. (2005). Windows evoke water themes. *Anglican Journal, 131,* 8.

Dreadfin Records & Clips. (2013, September 13). Orcas protected humans from sharks and saved drowning people. Retrieved from https://www.youtube.com/watch?v=r1ZkkHesyjg

Dr. Seuss. (2005). *The Cat in the Hat.* New York, NY: Random House.

Duncan, J. & Derrett, M. (1980). Ἦσαν γὰρ ἁλιεῖς (Mk. I 16): Jesus's fishermen and the parable of the net. *Novum Testamentum, 22*(2), 108–137.

Durkheim, E. (1995). *The Elementary Forms of the Religious Life.* Free Press: Washington, D.C.

Easton, M. G. (2005). Illustrated Bible Dictionary. New York, NY: Cosimo Classics.

Edinborough, A. (1987, September). Fish, not feasts, mainstay of New Testament menu. *Anglican Journal, 113*, 15.

Ehrenhalt, L. & Prachi S. (2016). *Jem* (TV, 1985). In *Pop Culture Universe: Icons, Idols, Ideas.* Santa Barbara, CA: ABC-Clio.

Eisenstadt v. Baird, 405 U.S. 438 (1972).

Ellis, L. (2014, November 26). More than 30 U.S. cities restricting food programs for homeless people. *The Christian Century, 131*, 16.

Endangered Species Act of 1973 (1973).

Euro News. (2010, July 25). A whale jumps on a boat in South Africa. Retrieved from https://www.youtube.com/watch?v=MOTGnizcP7g

Ewherido, A. O. (2006). *Matthew's Gospel and Judaism in the Late First Century C. E.: The Evidence from Matthew's Chapters on Parables (Matthew 13:1-52).* Peter Lang: New York, NY.

Favre, D. (2012). An international treaty for animal welfare. *Animal Law, 237*, 18.

Felton, J. E. (2006). R. E. story days. *Catechist, 40*, 46-47.

Finger, R. H. (2015, July). Jonah at sea. *Sojourners Magazine, 44*, 36-39.

Florida Fish and Wildlife Conservation Commission. (2015). General statewide bag and length limits. Retrieved from http://myfwc.com/fishing/freshwater/regulations/general/

Forbes, D. J. (2010). *A Christian apologetic to a Buddhist Christ* (Order No. 1474546). Available from Religion Database. (305240827).

Fowler, R. M. (1978). *Loaves and Fishes: The Function of the Feeding Stories in the Gospel of Mark (SBLDS 54).* Chico, CA: Scholars Press.

Francis, L. J. (2012). Interpreting and responding to the Johannine feeding narrative: An empirical study in the SIFT hermeneutical method amongst Anglican ministry training candidates. *Hervormde Teologiese Studies, 68*(1), 1-9.

Fraser, K. (2016, August 23). Killer whales hunting seal that jumps into boat. Youtube.com. Retrieved from https://www.youtube.com/watch?v=beZvsgqbMMQ

Frykholm, A. (2010, June 1). The theology of food: Eating and the eucharist. *The Christian Century, 127*, 39-40.

Galli, C. & Rise, P. (2009). Fish consumption, omega 3 fatty acids and cardiovascular disease. The science & the clinical trials. *Nutrition & Health, 20*(1), 11-20.

Gibbons, W. J. (2002). In search of the Congo dinosaur. Institute Creation Research. Retrieved from http://www.icr.org/article/search-congo-dinosaur

Gittins, A. J. (1994, September). Beyond hospitality? The missionary status and role revisited. *International Review of Mission, 83*, 397.

Goldfeder, M. & Sheff, E. (2013). Children of polyamorous families: A first empirical look. *Journal of Law & Social Deviance, 5*, 150-243.

Gonzales v. Carhart, 550 U.S. 124 (2007).

Goodhugh, W. & Taylor, W. C. (1943). *The Bible Cyclopædia: Illustrations of the Civil and Natural History of the Sacred Writings.* London, UK: Harrison & Co. Printers.

Green, J. B., Brown, J. K., & Perrin, N. (2013). *Dictionary of Jesus and the Gospels.* Madison, WI: InterVaristy Press.

Green, J. B., McKnight, S., & Marshall, I. H. (1992). *Dictionary of Jesus and the Gospels.* Downers Grove, IL: InterVarsity Press.

Gregg, R. C. (2015). *One Story, Three Ways Shared Stories, Rival Tellings: Early Encounters of Jews, Christians, and Muslims.* Oxford, UK: Oxford University Press.

Grove Press v. Christenberry, 276 F.2d 433 (1960).

Gulf Coast Exploreum. (2005). The Dead Sea Scrolls. Mobile, AL.

Habermas, J. (1987). *The Theory of Communicative Action.* Boston, MA: Beacon Press.

Halley, H. H. (2000). *Halley's Bible Handbook with the New International Version.* Grand Rapids, MI: Zondervan.

Hannah, B. (2006). *The Archetypal Symbolism of Animals: Lectures Given at the C. G. Jung Institute, Zurich, 1954-1958 (Polarities of the Psyche).* Ashville, NC: Chiron Publications.

Hanson, K. C. (1997). The Galilean fishing economy and the Jesus tradition. *Biblical Theology Bulletin 27,* 99-111.

Hauser, E. L. (2007, March 19). Saving the Jordan. *American Magazine.* Retrieved from http://www.americamagazine.org/issue/607/article/saving-jordan

Hawting, G. R. (1999). *The Idea of Idolatry and the Emergence of Islam: From Polemic to History.* Cambridge, UK: Cambridge University Press.

Heine, S. (2016). When there are no more cats to argue about: Chan Buddhist views of animals in relation to universal Buddha-nature. *Journal of Chinese Philosophy, 43.*

Hobbes, T. (2013). *Leviathan. The Project Gutenberg EBook.*

Hoehl, S. (2008). Empowered by Jesus: A research proposal for an exploration of Jesus' empowerment approach in John 21: 1-25. *The Journal of Applied Christian Leadership, 2*(2), 6-18. R

Hofman, E. G. (2003, January 17). A Sicilian feast. *Baltimore Jewish Times, 270,* 69.

HRS § 188-40.7 (2015).

Jaffe, M. (2008, February 29). Idols and atheists. *Baltimore Jewish Times, 301,* 13.

Jawad, L. A. (2006). Fishing gear and methods of the lower Mesopotamian plain with reference to fishing management. *Marina Mesopotamica, 1*(1), 1–37.

Jeffers, T. L. (2003). What remains of Robert Lowell? *Commentary, 116,* 59-66.

Jenkins, P. (2015, August 19). One story, three ways. *The Christian Century, 132,* 36-37.

Jensen, R. A. (1998, October). Dining in heaven. *Biblical Archeology Society, 14,* 32-39.

John, C. (n.d.). Salary per year for a crab fisherman. *Houston Chronicle.* Retrieved from
http://work.chron.com/salary-per-year-crab-fisherman-2510.html

Johnson, D. (2011). Eliciting an emotional response: An analysis of revenge and the criminal justice system. *Journal of Law & Social Deviance, 1,* 12-19.

Jung, C. G. (1991). The fish symbol is ambivalent. *Psyche and Symbol.* Princeton, NJ: Princeton University Press.

Katz, A. & Wrinn, C. (1996). *The Cat NOT in the Hat! A Parody by Dr. Juice.* London, UK: Penguin Books.

Keathley, J. H., III. (2004, May 26). Mark #4: A biblical concept of oneself. Bible.org. Retrieved from https://Bible.org/seriespage/mark-4-biblical-concept-oneself

Keulartz, J. (2015). Captivity for conservation? Zoos at a crossroads. *Journal of Agricultural & Environmental Ethics, 28*(2), 335-351.

Kingsley International Pictures Corp. v. Regents of the University of the State of New York, 360 U.S. 684 (1959).

Kirk, M. A. (1992). *Women of Bible Lands: A Pilgrimage to Compassion and Wisdom.* Collegeville, MN: Liturgical Press.

Kriz, T. (2014). Seven lies Christians tell. *Christianity Today.* Retrieved from http://www.christianitytoday.com/pastors/2014/february-online-only/seven-lies-christians-tell.html

Kuckro, R. (2014, June 30). Receding Lake Mead poses challenges to Hoover Dam's power output. E & E News. Retrieved from http://www.eenews.net/stories/1060002129

Kurlander, S. S. & Rakitt, S. A. (2013, March 21). Eat, enjoy, identify. *Washington Jewish Week.*

Las Vegas Valley Water District. (n.d.). Water Resources. Retrieved from http://www.lvvwd.com/about/wr.html

Lawrence, D. H. (1917). *Studies in Classic American Literature.* Retrieved from http://xroads.virginia.edu/~hyper/LAWRENCE/dhltoc.htm

--. (1971). “Whales Weep Not!,” New York, NY: Viking Penguin.

--. (2005). *Lady Chatterley's Lover.* Ware, UK: Wordsworth Editions.

Lawrence, R. J. (1991). The fish: A lost symbol of sexual liberation? *Journal of Religion & Health, 30*(4), 311-319.

Leon, H., et al. (2009). Effect of fish oil on arrhythmias and mortality: Systematic review. *British Medical Journal, 338*(7687), 149-152.

Lessem, D., Rowe, T., & Hammer, B. (n.d.). Unearthing dinosaur bones and fossils. Scholastic. Retrieved from http://www.scholastic.com/teachers/article/unearthing-dinosaur-bones-and-fossils

Lev-Yadun, S. (2009). Large-scale species introductions to preserve global biodiversity: Noah's ark revisited. *Ambio, 38*(3), 174.

Lindzon, J. (2015, April 22). I want to be a commercial fisherman. What will my salary be? *The Globe and Mail.* Retrieved from http://www.theglobeandmail.com/report-on-business/careers/career-advice/i-want-to-be-a-commercial-fisherman-what-will-my-salary-be/article24014591/

Lobsters Scream. (2007, April 26). Youtube.com. Retrieved from https://www.youtube.com/watch?v=m-sqpdL8anA

Lundin, S. C., Christensen, J., & Paul, H. (2002). *Fish Tales.* London, UK: Hodder & Stoughton.

Lyons, E. (n.d.). Have dinosaur and human fossils been found together? Apologetics Press. Retrieved from http://apologeticspress.org/APContent.aspx?category=9&article=4664

Machiela, D. A. & Perrin, A. B. (2014). Tobit and the genesis apocryphon: Toward a family portrait. *Journal of Biblical Literature, 133*(1), 111-132.

Magness, J. (2012). *The Archaeology of the Holy Land: From the Destruction of Solomon's Temple to the Muslim Conquest.* Cambridge, UK: Cambridge University Press.

Mare, W. H. (1987). *The Archeology of the Jerusalem Area.* Eugene, OR: Wipf and Stock Publishers.

Marrin, P. (2011). The paradox of Peter. *National Catholic Reporter, 47*(21), 17-22.

Martens, J. W. (2014). Share in the body. *America, 210,* 47.

Martin, H. V. (2014, October 5). God's gospel plan reaches communities. *Daily Press.*

Martin, J. B. (2007). The price of fame: CITES regulation and efforts towards international protection of the Great White shark. *George Washington International Law Review, 39,* 199-226.

McCullough, M. E., et al. (2016). Christian religious badges instill trust in Christian and non-Christian perceivers. *Psychology of Religion and Spirituality, 8*(2), 149-163.

McDonald, J. & Mumba, P. P. (2005). Nutrient composition of selected fresh and processed fish species from Lake Malawi: A nutritional possibility for people living with HIV/AIDS. *International Journal of Consumer Studies, 29*(1), 72-77.

McKay, B. & McKay, K. (2013, October 17). So you want my job: Commercial fisherman. The Art of Manliness. Retrieved from http://www.artofmanliness.com/2013/10/17/so-you-want-my-job-commercial-fisherman/

McKee, G. (n.d.). Killers of Eden. Ultimo, Australia: ABC Australia. Retrieved from http://www.killersofeden.com/

McLelland, J. (2009, July). Jesus in Islam. *The Presbyterian Record, 133,* 29-30.

McMinn, M. R., Staley, R. C., Webb, K. C., & Seegobin, W. (2010). Just what is Christian counseling anyway? *Professional Psychology: Research and Practice,41*(5), 391-397.

Melville, H. (1999). *Moby Dick.* Mienola, NY: Dover Publications.

--. (2005). *The Encantadas and Other Stories.* Mienola, NY: Dover Publications.

Miller, G. D. (2012). Raphael the liar: Angelic deceit and testing in the Book of Tobit. *Catholic Biblical Quarterly, 74*(3), 492-508.

Mittelbach, G. G., et al. (2014). Fish behavioral types and their ecological consequences. *Canadian Journal of Fisheries & Aquatic Sciences, 71*(6), 927-944.

Miyake, Y., et al. (2013). Fish and fat intake and prevalence of depressive symptoms during pregnancy in Japan: Baseline data from the Kyushu Okinawa maternal and child health study. *Journal of Psychiatric Research, 47*(5), 572-578.

Moeller, S. J. & Crocker, J. (2009). Drinking and desired self-images: Path models of self-image goals, coping motives, heavy-episodic drinking, and alcohol problems. *Psychology of Addictive Behaviors, 23*(2), 334-340.

Moore, P. (2011, June 16). Would you eat your friends? People for the Ethical Treatment of Animals (PETA). Retrieved from http://www.peta.org/blog/eat-friends/

Moroz, A. G. (2011). *Effective discipleship in central Virginia: Contextualizing the great commission in a changing southern culture* (Order No. 3444221). Available from Religion Database. (857921588).

Mulch, M. (2011, April 23). The hidden symbolism of fish in art. History of Painters. Retrieved from http://www.historyofpainters.com/fish.htm

Murphy-O'Connor, J. (1999). Fishers of fish, fishers of men: What we know of the first disciples from their profession. *Bible Review, 15*(3) 22-27, 48-49.

Noah's choice. (1995). *The Futurist, 29*(6), 40.

Noonan, B. J. (2011). Did Nehemiah own Tyrian goods? Trade between Judea and Phoenicia during the Achaemenid period. *Journal of Biblical Literature, 130*(2), 281-298.

Northup, L. A. (2006). Myth-placed priorities: Religion and the study of myth. *Religious Studies Review, 32*(1), 5-10.

--. (2008, October). Conversation with Dr. Lesley Northup. RLG 5025 Myth and Religion. Florida International University. Miami, FL.

Novick, T. (2007). Biblicized narrative: On Tobit and Genesis 22. *Journal of Biblical Literature, 126*(4), 755-764.

Nun, M. (1999). Ports of galilee. *Biblical Archaeology Review, 25*(4), 18-31

NY Stat. § 13-0338 (2014).

O'Brien, M. (2008). Reflections on the readings of Sundays and feasts June - August. *The Australasian Catholic Record, 85*(2), 233-252.

O'Hare, K. (2016, May 17). Sinead O'Connor, abortion, Lady Gaga and Catholicism — It's Complicated. Patheos. Retrieved from http://www.patheos.com/blogs/kateohare/2016/05/sinead-oconnor-abortion-lady-gaga-and-catholicism-its-complicated/

Oh, C. & Ditton, R. B. (2008). Using recreation specialization to understand conservation support. *Journal of Leisure Research, 40*(4), 556-573.

O. R. S. § 498.257 (2015).

-- § 509.160 (2015).

O'Sullivan, A. (2003). Place, memory and identity among estuarine fishing communities: Interpreting the archaeology of early medieval fish weirs. *World Archaeology, 35*(3), 449-468.

Parker, J. H. (1842). *Catena Aurea, Commentary on the Gospel of John, Collected of the Fathers by S. Thomas Aquinas*, Volume 4. London, UK: J. G. F. & J. Rivington.

People v. Dial Press, 182 Misc. 416, 48 N. Y. S. 2d 480 (N. Y. Magis. Ct. 1944).

Pérez Herrero, F. (2006, July). Mission following the missionary mandate of the risen Christ. *International Review of Mission, 95*, 306-319.

Pierce v. Society of Sisters, 268 U.S. 510 (1925).

Planned Parenthood v. Casey, 505 U.S. 833 (1992).

Planned Parenthood v. Danforth, 428 U.S. 52 (1976).

Podgurski, D. & Writer, S. (2004, July 18). *Advocate.*

Poudel-Tandukar, K., et al. (2011). Long chain n-3 fatty acids intake, fish consumption and suicide in a cohort of Japanese men and women--the Japan public health center-based (JPHC) prospective study. *Journal of Affective Disorders, 129*(1-3), 282-88.

Public Law 101–102 § 609 (1989).

Raji, C. A., et al. (2014). Regular fish consumption and age-related brain gray matter loss. *American Journal of Preventive Medicine, 47*(4), 444-451.

RCWA 77.15.770 (2014).

Redditt, P. L. (2007). Between text & sermon: John 19:38-42. *Interpretation, 61*(1), 68-70.

Reeves, J. (2009, December 18). Some in $4.6B Christian industry copy designs, logos. *USA Today*. Retrieved from https://usatoday30.usatoday.com/news/religion/2009-12-18-christian-copyright_N.htm

Rehmann, J. (2000). The historical-critical dictionary of Marxism: A Noah's ark of critical thinking. *Socialism & Democracy, 14*(2), 75-85.

Roark, M. L. (2007). Constitution as idea: Describing—defining--deciding in Kelo. *California Western Law Review, 43*, 363-387.

Robinson, E. (1838). *Biblical Researches in Palestine, mount Sinai and Arabia Petrea.* London, UK: A. Spottiswoode.

Robinson, E. & Smith, E. (2015). *Biblical Researches in Palestine and the Adjacent Regions.* Cambridge, UK: Cambridge University Press.

Roe v. Wade, 410 U.S. 113 (1973).

Roker, A. & Muth, C. R. (2011). *Coast Guard Alaska.* Atlanta, GA: The Weather Channel.

Ruge, A. & Marx, K. (1973). *Deutsch–Französische Jahrbücher.* Leipzig, Germany: Reclam.

Sanger, M. (2004). *The Autobiography of Margaret Sanger.* Mineola, NY: Dover Publications

Schaefer, G. O. & Savulescu, J. (2014). The ethics of producing in vitro meat. *Journal of Applied Philosophy, 31*(2), 188–202.

Schellenberg, R. S. (2011). Suspense, simultaneity, and divine providence in the book of Tobit. *Journal of Biblical Literature, 130*(2), 313-327.

Scott, S. M. (2016). Action figures. In *Pop Culture Universe: Icons, Idols, Ideas.* Santa Barbara, CA: ABC-Clio.

Seljak, D. (2001, March 26). Celebrating God's absence: Lent was a sombre and even oppressive time for a Catholic child growing up in the 1950s. *Canadian Mennonite, 5,* 6.

Share in Ramadan's mighty prayer. (2001). *National Catholic Reporter, 38*(5), 24.

Sharma, R. (2014). *Teach a Woman to Fish: Overcoming Poverty Around the Globe.* New York, NY: St. Martin's Press.

Shine, C. (2015, April 27). What Nevada has done to conserve water may serve as example for California. *Las Vegas Sun.* Retrieved from http://lasvegassun.com/news/2015/apr/27/tips-california-what-nevada-has-done-conserve-wate/

Sick, D. H. (2015). The symposium of the 5,000. *Journal of Theological Studies, 66*(1), 1.

Simpson, B. I. (2011). *A study of the historiographies of J. P. Meier and J. D. G. Dunn* (Order No. 3471022). Available from Religion Database. (885024098).

Smith, W. (1861). *A Dictionary of the Bible: Comprising Its Antiquities.* Boston, U.S.: Little, Brown and Company.

Smith, V. K. & Pattanayak, S. K. (2002). Is meta-analysis a Noah's ark for non-market valuation? *Environmental & Resource Economics, 22*(1-2), 271-296.

Snyder, M. (2012, April 21). Totems and animal symbolism. Retrieved from http://whiteknightstudio.blogspot.com/2012/04/totems-and-animal-symbolism.html

South, M. (1987). *"The Unicorn." Mythical and Fabulous Creatures: A Source Book and Research Guide.* Santa Barbara, CA: Greenwood Press.

Southern Nevada Water Authority (SNWA). (n.d.). Current Water Management. Retrieved from https://www.snwa.com/assets/pdf/wr_plan_exec_summary.pdf

Spencer, B. & Griffiths, S. (2014, December 3). Meet Sophie, the most complete stegosaurus skeleton ever found. *The Daily Mail.* Retrieved from http://www.dailymail.co.uk/sciencetech/article-2859296/Meet-Sophie-complete-stegosaurus-skeleton-found.html#ixzz4PQHEUXi0

Stacy, K. (2010). A pool of Torah. *Baltimore Jewish Times, 314*(8), 28-9.

Steenbrink, K. (2002). Jonah: From a prophetic mission in reverse to inter-religious dialogue. *International Review of Mission, 91*, 41-51.

Stendahl, J. (1998, January 28). The translation of wonder. *The Christian Century, 115*, 79.

Stevely, J. (2011, December 22). The deadliest job: Commercial fishing. *The Marine Science.* Retrieved from http://flseagrant.ifas.ufl.edu/newsletter/2011/12/the-deadliest-job-commercial-fishing/

Taking the Argo to Nineveh: Jonah and Jason in a Mediterranean. (1995). *Judaism, 44*(3), 341.

Tanner, A. (2007, August 21). Las Vegas growth depends on water supply. Environmental News Network. Retrieved from http://www.reuters.com/article/2007/08/21/environment-lasvegas-water-dc-idUSN133588232007082

Tanner, C. (2016, May 13). Bigotry, calls for violence, follow protest of tribal treaty fishing. Institute for Research & Education on Human Rights (IREHR). Retrieved from http://www.irehr.org/2016/05/13/bigotry-calls-violence-follow-protest-tribal-treaty-fishing/

Tennessee Fishing Guide (2016-2017). (2016). Tennessee Wildlife Resources Foundation and Tennessee Wildlife Resources Agency (TWRA). Knoxville, TN: The Bingham Group.

Texas Parks and Wildlife. (2015). Freshwater bag and length limits. Retrieved from https://tpwd.texas.gov/regulations/outdoor-annual/fishing/freshwater-fishing/bag-length-limits

The Economist. (2010, April 22). A new idolatry. Retrieved from http://www.economist.com/node/15954434

The Huffington Post. (2012, July 18). Shark fin ban challenged as discriminatory against Asians in new lawsuit. Retrieved from http://www.huffingtonpost.com/2012/07/18/shark-fin-ban-challenged-in-new-lawsuit_n_1684581.html

The St. Augustine Record. (2007, February 1). Ring story comes full circle. Retrieved from http://staugustine.com/stories/020107/sports_4373559.shtml#.WAVM0-ArLIU

The Times of Northwest Indiana. (2013, July 24). Flying silver carp on Wabash River in Indiana. NWITimes.com. Retrieved from http://www.nwitimes.com/news/opinion/columnists/guest-commentary/flying-silver-carp-on-wabash-river-in-indiana/youtube_04dcbd9c-9aae-56a1-83ba-492a4cb88d34.html

Toft, K. (2009, May 26). Killers in Eden. Public Broadcasting Service (PBS). Retrieved from http://www.pbs.org/wnet/nature/killers-in-eden-introduction/1048/

Troyer, J. (2010). *Discipleship in Mark: The development of followers* (Order No. 1485339). Available from Religion Database. (742430520).

United States Conference of Catholic Bishops (USCCB). (2016). The Book of Tobit: Tobiah's Return Journey to Nineveh and the Healing of Tobit (10:1–11:18). Retrieved from http://www.usccb.org/Bible/tobit/0

U.S. Department of Labor. (2014, January 8). *Occupational Outlook Handbook, 2014-15 Edition: Fishers and Related Fishing Workers.* Retrieved from http://www.bls.gov/ooh/farming-fishing-and-forestry/fishers-and-related-fishing-workers.htm.

U.S. Department of the Interior. (2013). Red Gulch dinosaur tracksite. Greybull, Wyoming.

--. (2015, March 12). Hoover Dam. Bureau of Reclamation. Retrieved from https://www.usbr.gov/lc/hooverdam/faqs/faqs.html

U.S. v. Stevens, 559 U.S. 460 (2010).

U.S. v. Washington, 520 F.2d 676 (9th Cir. 1975).

Van Den Eynde, S. (2005). One journey and one journey makes three: The impact of the readers' knowledge in the book of Tobit. *Zeitschrift Für Die Alttestamentliche Wissenschaft, 117*(2), 273-280.

V.T.C.A., Parks & Wildlife Code § 66.216-8 (2014).

--. § 66.2161 (2014).

Von Sadovszky, O. (1995). *Fish, Symbol and Myth.* Los Angeles, CA: International Society for Trans-Oceanic Research.

Wassell, B. E. & Llewelyn, S. R. (2014). "Fishers of humans," the contemporary theory of metaphor, and conceptual blending theory. *Journal of Biblical Literature 133*(3), 627-646.

Wax, H. (2007, May). Apes to man: Share food, make peace. *Science & Spirit, 18,* 12.

Weber, M. (2002). *The Protestant Ethic and the Spirit of Capitalism.* New York, NY: Penguin Books.

Weisheipl, J. A. (n.d.). *St. Thomas Aquinas, Commentary on the Gospel of St. John Part II: Chapter 21.* Albany, NY: Magi Books.

Weitzman, M. L. (1998). The Noah's ark problem. *Econometrica, 66*(6), 1279-1298.

Weitzman, S. (1996). Allusion, artifice, and exile in the hymn of Tobit. *Journal of Biblical Literature, 115*(1), 49-61.

Wells, T. (2000). The book of Revelation and the subject of worship. *Reformation & Revival 9*(3), 91-107.

Whale Wars. (2008). Season 1, Episode 1. Los Angeles, CA: Lizard Trading Company.

Whitbourne, S. K. (2012, July 28). Bragging, when is it ok and when is it not ok. *Psychology Today.* Retrieved from https://www.psychologytoday.com/blog/fulfillment-any-age/201207/bragging-when-is-it-ok-and-when-is-it-not-ok

Whitney, J. D. (2014, July 7). Corporate idolatry? Legal fictions don't have human rights. *American Magazine.* Retrieved from http://www.americamagazine.org/content/all-things/corporate-idolatry-legal-fictions-dont-have-human-rights

Wiarda, T. (2004). Scenes and details in the gospels: Concrete reading and three alternatives. *New Testament Studies, 50*(2), 167-184.

Winkel, T. (2015, November 15). Reward offered after invasive fish found in Swan Lake. NBC Montana. Retrieved from http://www.nbcmontana.com/news/-15K-reward-offered-after-invasive-fish-found-in-Swan-Lake/36468520

Wirpsa, L. (1998). Filipinos sing, share festive foods, teach old ways to young. *National Catholic Reporter, 34*(36), 3.

Woodworth, C. (2009). Picturing the Bible: The earliest Christian art. *Church History, 78*(3), 669-671.

World Trade Organization (WTO). (1998, November 6). United States — Import Prohibition of Certain Shrimp and Shrimp Products. WTO case Nos. 58 (and 61). Retrieved from https://www.wto.org/english/tratop_e/envir_e/edis08_e.htm

Yick Wo v. Hopkins, 118 U.S. 356 (1886).

Youtube.com. (2007, March 31). Marlin stabbing. Retrieved from https://www.youtube.com/watch?v=D2NvLPGDV5c

Youtube.com. (2016, May 3). Dolphin accidentally jumps into boat. Retrieved from https://www.youtube.com/watch?v=mP8LYOHrPbc

Zucker, D. (1995). Jonah's journey. *Judaism, 44*(3), 362.

Index

O

P

Q

R

S

T

V

W

Z

www.ingramcontent.com/pod-product-compliance
Lightning Source LLC
Chambersburg PA
CBHW072144020426
42334CB00018B/1876

* 9 7 8 1 6 2 2 7 3 2 3 5 7 *